A LITTLE BIT OF EVERYTHING
ALL WRAPPED UP INTO ONE MESSY BOOK OF UNHINGED CHAOS

CALLISTO & MOON
PUBLISHING

a little bit of everything
all wrapped up
into one messy book
of unhinged chaos

Printed in the United States

NYC Skyline Design illustrated by Michelle / Instagram:
@_kb.cardi

ISBN – 979-8-9863313-1-7
Find more pieces of work from K. La Lune
@ k.la_lune ; www.iamklalune.com

ALSO BY K. LA LUNE

Mirror, Mirror
She Loves Me, She Loves Me Not

A LITTLE BIT OF EVERYTHING
ALL WRAPPED UP INTO ONE MESSY BOOK OF UNHINGED CHAOS

k. la lune

CALLISTO & MOON
PUBLISHING

ACKNOWLEDGMENTS

Ever since I was a little girl, *I knew* I wanted to be a writer. Hell! I'd even say that I knew I was *destined* to be.

As a child (an only child), I relied on myself and this rich sprouting blossom of creativity to keep me company. I never had many friends and it *never* bothered me. I was always in the embrace of my own magnetic imagination, crafting storylines for movies- putting on shows with my Barbie's.

"*Peculiar*," they would say; *they*- my parents and their friends. I was always a bit "strange and unusual;" always feeling the need to dress different, talk different, and emulate a new version of myself that didn't yet exist.

I was a story-teller, making up the most absurd tales, thinking it was normal to pretend they were real, because to me, *they were*. I'd sketch words in my head; words that no 8-year-old would know or understand. *But, that's just it*;

These words, phrases, stories- they come to me in drifts of thoughts and visions. I don't need to have ever seen or heard certain words before, nor cognitively understand their meanings. I just feel and then I release them through ink onto pages.

My mind has always been a crash course for chaos- a field of dreams with a nuance of unexpected ideas; both spry and lithe, quixotic and untamed.

Understanding that there was a way, a place, in which I could share my gift and love for writing with others, changed my life completely. Once I was aware that the contents of my mind could be displayed amongst pages of books and filled in libraries and bookstores, I was a menace on the hunt, pouring extra flavor into every tonic of creativity I'd serve to others along the way.

If it wasn't for her, I don't think I would have ever picked up a pen and paper again; burying my soul purpose six feet under, never to taste the visceral knowing of what it is that I'm destined to do.

My writing, much like my mind, is wordy. But, that's exactly how I like it. I thank all those who have supported my work and made it possible for me to stay encouraged to keep my dream alive- to forever strengthen this muscle of talent; many thanks and many blessings.

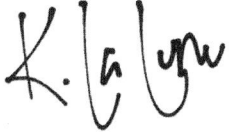

contents

OF A CHAOTIC MIND

WARNING TO THE READER

This book contains mature subject material that may be
disturbing or upsetting, including sex, drugs & alcohol, death,
depression, and distorted body image.
Reader discretion is advised.

for all the souls
who have, *perfectly*,
found mine

Thank you.

undone but not finished

Many of these pieces may feel "undone" and "incomplete"
because in a lot of ways, *they are*. I'm a believer in things coming
full circle- that a single moment is never truly gone; that fate
will always bring it back around, someway/somehow. I like to
look at these pieces as preludes to the grand enthrall to their
endings, dressing them in undergarments, fitting them for their
marvelous grand exit, while enjoying the simplistic rush within a
fleeting moment of *chaos*.

If you're uncomfortable with any of the topics that have been
outlined on previous pages, I would strongly suggest
reconsidering reading. My aim is to share my voice, my
experiences, and my mind with the world- to set these words
free to run wild into the hearts of those they're meant to touch.

Thank you for being here.

I'm not the kind of artist to simplify their words or compact them into tiny neat little sections for the world to understand and try to dissect. The contents of this book are *scattered, chaotic, and undeniably messy* because I too, am all of those things. I write from a place of pure thrill, chasing a nuance of impulsive sensations; the kind that furrow behind my spine, making a home for their emotive state of being. I'm a vessel for undeniable treasures- spoonful's of words ready to explode from the seams, loosely stitched and threaded together by golden twine, ignited by the midnight sun.

Sure, I could have folded and piled the themes into their own cute compartments; easily sorted, a perfect guide to abridged reading, but then, that wouldn't be an accurate depiction of who I am and how the workings of this wild mind ride;

autopilot.

These themes co-exist under a penumbra of disheveled moments- messy, unhinged, and a bit too honest for some people to enjoy.

As my age continues to ripen, I become more keen to the key of human complexity- that it's not black nor white. The color palette is far too advanced for the soul to compute and understand.

I'm easily tempted and stricken with endless curiosity; feeding both the light and dark sides of a wandering soul, behaving in lieu with a human mind, whose control is unmatched by a perplexing range of emotions. I'm a walking juxtaposition, from my third eye to the unmatched socks on my feet.

I live in a constant state of bewilderment, unearthed by my own mind battling with this fluttering organ pumping unworldly words throughout my blood- a maddened game of tug of war, pulling me from one thought to the next, while I'm on a rollercoaster, changing speeds of emotion quicker than the ride itself.

And yet, I remain [unapologetic]. I don't fit inside of society's manufactured structures, nor do I abide by poetry's classical stanza's, sonnets, or formats. Like me, my writing is rebellious, strange, wordy, and imperfectly disruptive in all the right ways.

And with that, *I hope you stay.*

isle of reckless things

isle of reckless things | the nuclei of chaos

"DO IT ANYWAY"

I know I shouldn't but I lack the ability to harness the agility of self-control; wrapping the consequence in cellophane to ditch amidst a barren corner of my mind; where cycles of misery and thought provoking adversaries are left to wither, urging me to dump the thoughts and "*casually*" forget.

I'm too keen on letting my soul breathe, chasing emotional peril with googly eyes and wishful envy- a shoddy excuse for my actions to lay limp across my morals, granting me the gift of self-persuasion;

"*not to worry, do it anyway.*"

I JUST DON'T GIVE A F*%K

I used to care what people thought of me

as I'd allow my own mistakes

when seen through their eyes,

to keep me tethered in place

when I only wanted to escape.

Flames would fulminate around me

and I'd shout as loud as I could

for someone to help

get me out of this mess, this elaborate stress.

Pounce on me, break these chains,

feed me validation that everything

would be okay

in order to force my way

through the burns along the way.

Time would come and time would go,

elapsing faster than I'd ever known.

And somehow, these people and their enemies

could no longer get to me.

It's then I realized the most important thing-

that the only person who could free me, *was me.*

THE WOMAN WHO COULDN'T SEE, SAW ME

While riding the subway, a frail woman is staring and I begin to shift uncomfortably. With eyes as hazy and dull as the fog on a window after a rainstorm, she tries to communicate. My heart rate begins to rise, pulsating in rhythm to the clamor of the wheels on the tracks.

For some time, I had looked down at the book in my lap, hoping she'd focus her attention elsewhere while counting the stops until I could get off next.

Still, I can feel the heat cast from her direction, watching me with purposeful intent. And when I look up again, she's still staring with a wash of worry now shrouding her face.

I'm only two stops away and I'd rather walk a few extra blocks than to riddle myself with anxiety any longer. Packing my belongings, I begin to rise from my seat, but it feels like an extra few pounds of gravity is holding me in place.

I glance back over at the woman and she hasn't taken her gaze away from me. It's then that the subway comes to a screeching halt- the outside world veiled in darkness as the train holds its breath underneath the tunnel.

You've got to be joking.

After much hesitation, the frail woman approaches, ushering me to sit back down. While in her presence, her soul feels warm, her aura is comforting, and my heart begins to relax. Those washed-out eyes couldn't see, but somehow, they *saw me.*

Bowing her head, she grabs my hand, and thanks me. "*I'm sorry, I don't think I know you,*" I say at last as my eyes wander around the train, wondering how no one else noticed what was happening.

Beginning to speak rapidly and in a different tongue, she removes paper from a sketchbook in her bag and begins to draw, while looking up at me ever-so-often to see if I understand.

The black ink bleeds through to the other side of the paper and she holds up the drawing of a stick figure. I shake my head, confused.

Swiftly, she tears the page so it splits the figure in half and proceeds to draw two more figures. Next, she places one piece of the split figure on top of figure two and the other on top of figure three. It's then that I understand.

I swallow hard. *But how does she know?*

"*You must believe, chosen one,*" she whispers, gripping my hands with her frail cold fingers. I nod, mystified.

Releasing me, the subway begins to move and when I turn my head back around, the woman is gone- vanished into the lost abyss of an unknown.

PUPPET

Maneuvered by strings attached to my limbs,

I walk as they say

and say as they do.

Dressed from head to toe in what

the world seems to think fits best,

I walk in shoes that are too small or too big.

"Smile!"

"Say yes!"

"Do this,"

"but, don't do that."

Morbidly fatigued as I fit in to appease

the ill-needy society.

My words are procured from a book,

like reading off a teleprompter,

careful not to say too much

because, that just "wouldn't look good."

Tryingly taught to hate,

I'm silenced by the puppeteers-

the ones who'd rather watch me fall than speak my truth

as steel-bulleted restraints cover my mouth

and threaten to ruin me if I do.

GET ON YOUR KNEES AND PRAY

Rock bottom, *we meet again.* I'm not surprised to see you- we all know misery is my biggest fan. Let's grab a coffee and catch up. Since last time, I've lost another job, as well as all my friends. Lost my car, tons of money, my sanity even.

I'm numb beyond saving grace; fought a battle, lost that too… I'm almost thirty, *fuck dude.* Still not married, nope, no kids yet. I don't know what I'm waiting for, stop asking me that!

Still haven't moved to LA, maybe one day. No, I'm not procrastinating! Now, you're just assuming. But, enough about me, what about you?

Excuses? me? I'm not wallowing in pity, just privy to knowledge, so, I go with the flow. Driven in circles, I bruise over speedbumps.

They tell me to get on my knees and pray, hoping I'd be saved from the never-ending story of a clandestine fate.

A SPIRITUAL AWAKENING

For once, I'm at a loss for words- my tongue is at the mercy of a silent curving of unknowns, keeping me lost within a sea of outrageous tides, pulling gravity in every direction I turn. Unable to mold what I feel into tangible understanding, I drown amidst these outlandish feelings that perpetuate deeper questioning.

DOWN THE RABBIT HOLE

I fell in love too fast- plummeting down a rabbit hole and past the skies into a ruthless oblivion; a cloud I'd sit upon, watching stars saunter by, bypassing every wish I'd make to see you again. I fell in love with someone who I knew could never love me back- a repelling afterthought splaying chaos like acidic backwash, drowning me in wonderments that would never see the light of day.

THAT'S THE THING ABOUT SOBRIETY

I once sold my soul to a fine glass of French 75, carving my name into the binding contract poured down my throat- an elixir of false confidence and foreboding repercussions. Late nights and monstrous mornings were just the tip of the iceberg during business hours. Every Friday into Sunday morning, I was tied to my obligation of being "that girl."

You know, the "fun girl,"

> "always down for a good time, girl,"
> "blackout on a Friday night, girl."

And one day, things just… changed. I was tired of being "that girl-" the one who always found herself in predicaments that lowered her self-worth. So, I forced myself off the wagon, which turned out easier than anticipated. Clarity reigned a new beginning- colored vision returning as the once dull world around me flourished with divine effervescence.

No longer clouded by looming shadows aberrating my judgment, my innermost soul thanked me for its freedom, now pardoned from a space of captivity. I yearn for deeper meanings, losing myself in lucid visions, viewing life through a new lens- one of unconditional kindness, patience, and forgiveness.

EXPIRATATION DATE

Lately, I worry about
my shelf life-
wondering how much time
I have left to do all
the things on this never-ending
bucket list.
It's a taxing thought
that keeps me hibernating
in this cave,
too afraid that if I step
the wrong way,
I'll succumb to my fate.
I think too much
about how many seconds
I have left to live,
as I coil my lifeline around
the minute hand
of the clock.
I hang in limbo
from around the hour,
slowly watching time tick by,
while I grow older
and closer to my demise.
Unhealthy,
I know and I pray that it changes-
that maybe one day,
I'll no longer cower behind fear,
but yet, *fear will cower behind me.*

K. LA LUNE

AN INSATIABLE CRAVING FOR A BROKEN HEART

Crazy, I know, but I have an insatiable appetite for a broken heart. I know that I'm different, feeling things more profoundly than most- accepting and welcoming to a myriad of endless ranges of emotion.

When it rains, I beg for it to pour- to coast along with the droplets that match the ones falling from my eyes. I'll rush to a cliff at Gods speed, halting just as my feet touch the edge, my heart catching in my throat.

I chase the very things that I know I'll never have, but still do just so I can emerge from the dawn, beaming with bliss- just for reality to pedal in, leaving me to crumble and sink amidst my own mess.

I'll curl amongst the floor, my backbone just as exposed and cold as my soul starving for warmth- hand clutched at my chest, fixed on the euphoric agony that knows my name better than any.

I'm a deity for tragedy, a politician for endless possibilities.

RUBY RED SLIPPERS

If I could surmise a way to click
my heels three times over,
I'd wish my way to a land

beyond the rainbow,

where colors flood the sky above,
catching dreams of a lifetime
as I stick out my tongue.

LOOKING FOR EVERAFTER

I waver somewhere in a limbo state of mind; where the past and present co-exist amid a stark bandwidth made with conniving hits of juxtapositions- dark and light comparisons of who I "*was*" and who I "*am*."

When signaling for a sign, I allow these bruised knees to come clean, pleading with sky bombed anomalies to stretch me open, gifting insight to what it is that these tired hands are destined to touch, meant to change, meant to nullify and rearrange.

I'm gut punched and weepy, surrendering my white flag, trading chaos for peace, and these gold stars for a second chance- a possible happy ever after buried with these once in a lifetime treasures;

> a key that hides in between the hollowed spaces of my teeth- forthcoming when I allow my strength to speak.

TEMPLE OF THE SOUL

I keep myself stretched open,
allowing butterflies and moon dust
to free fall from these skeletal fixtures,
holding my instrument
for loving taut behind its grips.

Keen on the intricacy
of how each note within me sings,
I bind the most precious sentiments
to an oath,
strung by silver lake string,
and laced tight
amongst diamond-embellished gates-

an energetic aura encased
around the heart
of all that I am and all that

I'm destined to be.

ZONING OUT

I'm zoned out, flood-filled eyes focused on a passing of time, where memories fester, and I'm left with nothing; nothing but a welcoming ache that I crave, *no, that I need to feel*- the kind that dwells beneath the coves from which my heart still swims freely in, allowing the water to enter my ears and drown out the noise- reminding me of the silence that always seems to follow after a storm.

I'm subdued in the mindless chatter of prophetic daydreams; catching seedlings of what's yet to procure from these visions. For these eyes are a gift, a conduit, connecting spirit to the core pitted at the forefront of my being; echoes of the stars that sing in lulling harmonics- rich in saccharine wonderments bewitching me from afar.

POETIC AGONY KILLED THE POET

They ask me if it's *love*; if your honey suckle eyes live up to the words I've stained amongst their minds- ruby delicious flavor gushing from the seams that hold the beautiful rhymes inside of you.

They're curious of the tides that keep me submerged so far under; bewildered by my agility to hold my breath for so long, even when the roaring waters fill my lungs and wither me into a unremembered void of nothing.

Little do they know how poetic the agony really is- how my lungs don't lose air, yet expand with gardens of visions sparking wildly, reviving me of all hope lost, birthing new-found faith in a clandestine kind of way.

RED PILL OF SHAME

I'm used to fucking up;
that sometimes I
even get so drunk where
I end up in strange places,
unable to feel my feet
or move my face.
Yeah,
that's how bad it gets.
I'd blackout on the hard stuff-
achy bones and memory loss
come morning
as I'd drag myself to the car,
walking in disgrace.
"You're a fucking idiot"-
yeah, me.
There's dozens of no name
phone numbers
buzzing me relentlessly,
thanking me for a crazy night.
The fuck did I do.
Does it matter?
I'm still mad at you-
a resentment so vile
that at times, I self-sabotage
and numb away the pain.

K. LA LUNE

But, I'm only hurting myself.
I'm a monster,
handcrafted, homemade, and painted
by none other than you.
You made me this way-
taught me all your ways to
keep myself bound
within the chokehold
of a disastrous party scene,
as shards of glass pinned me in place,
keeping me scathed
and detached
while you left without a trace.
Untouched, unhinged,
lecturing me on how to better
take care of the mess,
in order to eliminate *your* stress.
You fucking bitch.
Force-fed a red pill of shame-
jagged edges, I swallow your hypocrisy
of "don't let it happen again."
So, I pillow myself comfortably,
and lay like a cushion between your teeth-
washed away as they bleed.

BLACKED OUT ON THE 7:56 EXPRESS

It could go without saying- "*I had too much.*" Five French 75's and a few tequila shots later, memories of that late afternoon became submerged underneath a poison sinking my lucidity under. The timeline of events roam my mind in patches, still foggy without much detail to help the investigation.

___ paisley maxi dress
___ favorite pair of sunglasses (now lost and gone for good)
___ braided ponytail
___ meeting V at the rooftop bar at 2:00 PM

So far, so good.
I can still recall the vehement rays from the sun absorbing into my skin while I drank the first glass of champagne and gin. We sat parallel to the Empire State Building, almost making eye contact with the tippy-top as we drank.

Around 4:00 PM is when things became hazy as I promised myself that last drink was actually "the last" because I was 'two-sheets-to-the-wind' by then. *Of course, that wasn't the case.* I remember most of what had transpired next but some parts I'm still unsure of.

___ elevator down to the lobby (it started raining, I remember)
___ sitting in the Uber (not sure how I got in there)
___ explaining to V that I'm "*totally fine, I'm just meeting a friend*"
___ somehow walking back to the rooftop bar
___ waiting in the lobby (again)

K. LA LUNE

__ (drunken) texts that outlined where I was and what I was wearing

__ sitting back on the rooftop with another glass of French 75 and some tequila shots (now with a different friend) - (seriously, how did I get back up there?)

Consequently, I became a different person while under the influence of Mr. French, which made "future me" facilitate cleaning the mess of the beating this version of me took.

"Are you sure you're fine?" my friend asked as I stumbled over stories that probably didn't make any sense.

Now, we're really heading into oblivion territory, where my memory only lives within that moment, unable to procure the elixir to remember.

"You have such a cute apartment!" I said with the kind of drunken-enthusiasm you'd absolutely expect from someone who just downed five glasses of champagne and gin, alongside however many shots of tequila within the span of three hours.

"I think you should go home," he mutters as he forces a giant glass of water into my system. "You've had enough for the day."

"I'm finNnNnNeEeE!" I squeal, reluctantly able to remember the feeling of being rejected as I consented to whatever it is that I can't remember. "Actually, can I use your bathroom?" I asked, watching the room vacillate on the highest speed setting as my vision blurred every color and thing in the room together.

The porcelain toilet seat kept me grounded while my stomach argued with the extra alcohol invading its space. I was spinning faster than I was before, unable to keep my head on straight as I panicked about how I was getting home *in this state.*

Making our way down, *a seemingly*, endless amount of stairs, I kept falling (inside of my head), failing to see what was right in front of me. As we'd reached the subway turnstile, I fumbled amongst my bag for my metro card as my heart rate increased when I realized I had "lost it."

[That isn't the only thing you lost. Don't forget your sunglasses (which you'd realize days later) and your mind (which has failed you in making safe decisions).

"Here, I'll swipe you through," my friend offered, running his metro through. "You sure you're okay to get back uptown?" he asked, talking to a void in the system of my human identity, now lost in the translation of non-sobriety.

I must have said yes because somehow I managed to get off one subway and onto the correct connecting one as I headed towards Penn Station. Not only that, but I'd even gotten myself onto the right express train heading home.

From panicking at the downtown subway station to the next morning, laying in my own sweat and murky thoughts, I have no recollection of the time that elapsed between then.

I ran to the mirror, pinching myself to make sure I was really there because my brain couldn't think or process or remember much of anything. The last thing I really recalled, in that moment, was being on the rooftop with V.

What a terrifying shock- to wake up on a new day in my bed with no memory to validate "*how* or when." As I rushed to my mirror, I noticed my makeup was missing as I stared at a clean-washed face. I don't even remember getting home or showering.

For hours, I was a walking-breathing void, blacked-out while talking, thinking, walking, behaving in ways that I'll never remember. *And something about that was deeply unsettling.*

Looking back now, a few years later, I consider myself extremely lucky and blessed that I made it back safely while hibernating in an aloof-struck shell that controlled me.

If I hadn't learned my lesson then, the "next time", I might have not been as *lucky*.

her

her | *the eternal one*

ETERNAL BOND OF FOREVER

The silence was deafening, but loud enough to pierce pins through the vacuum of stillness, puncturing the already fractured hope deflating inside my chest.

I'd procure every word ever written by man, to serve to her like a 4-course dinner meal; poetic psalms to ignite her palette as though she were under a spell.

I was in debt to the sun from all the brightness I'd borrowed, to banish the shadowing darkness that devoured me in angst along the way.

From *my lips to the moons ears*, I'd offer love notes in exchange for her secrets, spilling all of the contents sloshing around inside of me, bargaining for a voice to show me the way forward.

When the sleepless nights met the light of day, I'd deface any surface with the initials of her name, solidifying our fate in the eternal bond of forever.

I think of you all hours of the day- even when my eyes close and drift towards the western summit of my dreams.

I think of your skin and how lovely it feels when brushed against mine- its velveteen touch; a perfect canvas for art.

I think of your eyes and how they grow and shrink in size; symbolic of the changing seasons of your life.

I run through a gamut of scenarios and conversations that we'll have, gardening and tending to the most poetic words to feed your soul.

I water them daily with each sprinkling of hope that washes over after a storm has passed, hanging on to the wishes I hold in the sky, nursing its innocence in each day that passes, and all of the stars that promise me they listen.

PROMISE NEVER KEPT

A promise

    never kept

        were words

            you never meant-

allowing the lie to curl beneath the truth,
hovering in plain sight;

an ugly rhyme too blind to take notice,
while under the influence of nightmarish sweet nothings

        that bubble at the fold of a lover's lips;
        the poisonous kiss to feed a craving once starved,
        for just one taste will keep you wistful long enough.

MIRAGE OF THE NIGHT

Woken in layers of sweat pooled around my skin, I gasp for air, grasp the sheets strangling reality, keeping me trussed to the in-between; an alarming space where my lucidity remains paralyzed amidst the daunting messages following me intently.

I'm

drifting

further away from this place as my eyes begin to open, stretching my arms to reach the mirage of your fairly remembered ghost, unable to leave before you've said your peace- the truth dancing on the tip of your tongue while you watch me leave, until the next time we meet.

ONWARD AND UPWARD TO OBLIVION

Trick of the light, I'm bonded to a wayward dreamscape whisking me away, carrying me towards the outskirts of your heart. I'm tucked between the outside world *and* the lens of how you see me, feeling around for any clues that have escaped under your control;

> a regime of stoic fears standing guard at a pinnacle of a doorway that'll lead me to you.

With one twist of the key, I've stepped upon the clouds that cushion your mind; where the stars cradle your darkest wishes in a silky embrace.

Just when I think I've captured your eyes, you fade to ash, and I wither to dust- slipping away like sand in an hourglass; like nightfall kissing dusk.

A MOMENT WORTH WAITING FOR

My mouth's gone dry–

once bountiful words

that spurred with wildflowers,
now hardened and withered
at the base of my shoes.

There's a mass of letters
stacked high amongst my heart,
inked and sealed
with each letter of your name;

silent wishes

that sit beside shattered dreams,
wilting as each day fades
into another year
spent waiting for you.

K. LA LUNE

HAUNTED BY UNSPOKEN TRUTHS

Three years later, I've remained haunted by your eyes- the way they held mine in a guarded stance, unwavering to allow me in; a distant response altered from their habitual honeysuckle charm, pushing me as far away as these state lines that now divide our bodies apart.

Since then, time has eaten away at the memory, scoffing up tidbits of that day- loud reminders of moving lips and silent tongues; words I hid in spite of fear, to hold hostage in the hollows, collecting a gamut of cobwebs over the years;

a punishment so cruel, bellowing deep from inside these bones, holding galaxy sized teardrops behind curious eyes and a quivering jaw; awaiting to puncture and release a storm of a million, "I *love you's*" feigning to escape formidable control.

FORGET ME NOT

Like a forget me not

rupturing through a crack in the sidewalk,

wrapping pleas worth of memories around your ankles,

I'm hopeful that the taste of my words

still linger in your mind,

and warm your heart

for *many more years and many more nights.*

A BLUR IN TIME

In passing time, your face blurs through this window of my mind; a faceless memory starving for one more moment to stand beside you, feeling sunbeams dance through my core from just one look behind your starry eyes; moonlight carving prayers into my bones, shaking as they grow tired, grow older.

The old woman on the train once told me that magic stirs wildly in the tips of my fingers- that I have the power to turn all things lost in exile into summits of gold.

Still, I've saved that touch for your hand to hold, hoping for a second chance to find us- a time in space where I'd be able to change your mind, giving faith to this cosmic knowing of fate.

.

\

A DAY IN JULY

It's true- I never thought I'd see her again as my arms wrapped around her delicate frame, *for what I initially believed*, was the last time.

Those final seconds felt even shorter as my mind complicated time, fighting with metaphorical hands pulling me away. My heart was robust in all the right things, having sewn and stitched my words, perfectly tailored to her taste- and yet, these seconds were *still, somehow*, stolen away- as limp as my tongue being buried beneath her gravity.

The nights that followed agonized my entirety, hanging me by the choice of all I left unsaid; where my words once murmured atop a pinnacle of my chest, now beginning to plummet, drowning where all wishes fail to rise- a subsequent consequence of my demise.

LOCKET

For years, I wore her like a locket, pulling at the imaginary welding that bonded my lifeline to hers, soothing the persistent menace that grappled for my attention- a declaration of clandestine signs that beckoned for me to *listen*;

> *listen* to the voice showering me with wisdom; emergence of my soul purpose and the everlasting promise of our cosmic affair from a distance.

AS IF I COULD FORGET YOU

As if I could forget you- I'm fixed in your orbit; rising like the sun, setting like the moon, carved amidst your map. Even when I run, you're still there- haunting my thoughts in the face of white noise beveled above my head.

There's no escape as I reach for a door… *any door.* Most of them remain locked and gated. The ones that seem to open lead me right back into the magnetic enthrall of your being.

When I close my eyes, it's your hand that's rested upon my cheek, whispering chilling secrets that bruise and bring me to my knees.

These words are sickly sweet; a poisonous flavor that revives me for only a few minutes, until its reality sinks beneath my tongue like a soot-infused and blackened tonic, hastening the decay of this heart's cycle of breaking.

NO TIME BUT DIVINE TIME

It's not that I believe that time slipped, pocketing a portal where destiny fell through the cracks, rushing our fate before the stars aligned at the perfect time.

No- I'm certain that day has been written in our blueprint for ages;

serendipitously

mapped and gaged for a moment that no deficit could impede.

On the taxi downtown, I just knew that something felt *unusual-* precariously on edge, yet enthralled with the euphoric sense that something was brewing beyond the bright indigo skies.

My heart thundered, climbing like a symphony of violins, perplexed by the sudden fullness erupting at the center of my chest as I approached the coordinates of fate that have been laced within our blood for eternity.

The angels sang, leading me to you- to sit with the clamoring strike of "familiarity" that would hit instantaneously upon catching my eye.

And, there you were- a vision in blue; sparkly and perfectly imperfect from a distance.

ALL THE RIGHT WAYS

She's my mirror.

Without fault, her strengths subdue my flaws, keeping them buoyant at even keel when lightning strikes too close to home, absolving disaster rearing its cataclysmic charm.

She runs, I chase.

> a never ending battle of right person, wrong time, fooling our soul-bound lifelines, twisting their strings and clumping chaos at the knot drifting us apart.

But still, *I have hope*; hope in the idyllic synastry of core energy, reminding me of her love when I need it most- that these redolent waves of grandeur speak in a language kissed by the stars; ready to cast each wish a grant, a promise... that you never have to look any further than the subtle whisper of your own soul.

INTERLUDE

I'D WAIT A MILLION MORE LIFETIMES FOR US TO "**GET IT RIGHT**"-

ALLOW THE *stars* TO

CALL ME HOME EACH TIME.

WHILE YOU SLEEP

Whispers tickle my ear,

mocking what used to be.

I wake from my sleep *(or so I think),*

jolting forward as I search

for a strange familiar.

The room in its entirety is empty,

aside from the tangible oddities surrounding me.

My arms wrap around my body

while my hands cup my mouth,

careful not to let any weeping escape.

It's all an imprudent facet of a plagued reality,

beckoning me to live this nightmare,

even when I'm asleep.

The ache finds me in my most

vulnerable state of mind-

humming obscurities as she visits me in my dreams.

Tonight's a rough one.

A torrent of memories surge through the threshold-

serrated edges of a once happy ever after

seep somewhere deep inside.

A choppy storm of dejection in its utmost state of cruelty,

finds a way to diminish any progress of healing wounds.

The past surges through

the peaks and valleys of my heart,

relentlessly mocking what used to be,

reminding me of a once perfect dream- the *A team.*

A serendipitous duo of unapologetic youth.

K. LA LUNE

WHEN THE FEELINGS HIT

It hit me like the dead weight of a cinder block,

jolting reasoning from its ruin of habit.

She carved me out,

leaving nothing,

not even scraps

to piece myself

back together.

THIRTY SOMETHING

I'm inching closer; pleading with God to halt time; to delay this cosmic dance around the sun, for I'm not ready to watch my face decay with age- not ready to say goodbye to the catharsis of my youth.

Still, there's hope when I look into your eyes and see myself in the window of your heart; bright-eyed and poetically lithe; porcelain skin and an untamed tongue failing to silence after being bitten one too many times.

Because… you see… with you, *I'm infinite*; beguiled in the paradigm of everlasting existence- a forever home where I'm safe in the hands of memory; a place I'll visit right before blowing out the last standing candle on this 30-ish something birthday.

WARM LIKE HONEY

Your eyes are like warm honey-

decadent and sultry.

their allure tells a story of their own,

dispelling everything without saying anything.

LIFETIMES

For lifetimes,

I've been loyal to one heart,
shooing away the lot who beckoned for my attention.

For lifetimes,

I was a writer,
filling the earth with her initials
and all the intangible wishes that came along with it.

SECRETS OF A STARRY NIGHT

Without warning, she moves through the mystical static that weaves reality and someplace far; a landscape that houses both nightmares and dreams.

Tonight, she's ignited my sweet tooth,

tearing through me with the softest voice, whispering all the golden treasures I feign to hear;

> but only when my eyes close and my hands rest- only able to touch what human hands can't; spectral pieces of outside lands that conspire with one another to bring us together.

RUIN OF EXILE

There's endless budding curiosities that lie beneath her touch; a ruin of exile burying all that's left unsaid to wallow in the dirt.

> Withering lungs, half-beaten and bruised, she's a pawn to the façade- disillusioned in the unfulfilling deceptions that barely keep her afloat; a ceaseless wave that drowns her before crashing at the shore.

12 HOURS IN A DAY

With her, I'm *limitless* and time is a *frazzled existence*; both non-existent mixed with a whiplash sort-of haste; almost as if there are only 12 hours in a day, where the sun and the moon never part, only touch and become one.

That's what being with her is like.

RUNNING THROUGH THE FOREST (FOREST OF FEARS)

I'm running through the forest with bare feet, dirt caked at the soles, in search of the distant half of my own. She's somewhere in the thrush of evergreens that cascade around the trees, hiding from the chase- exalting jamborees blaring throughout her head; a curiosity that starves when in the presence of fear.

I call her name with the tranquil sonata that drips from my tongue- a sound that only she can hear. But, she's silenced by an obscure view of what binds her to the disassociation of letting my love in.

ONLY A WISH AWAY

I always think about what it'd be like to see you again- envisioning every detail, hyperaware of each stitch poking loose from its seam. I imagine your face and the expression that would rise as I entered the room;

> *would you be happy to see me?*

> *Shocked?*

> *Shy?*

> *Maybe even a nuance of fear*
> *strumming beneath your bones,*
> *rattling them raw?*

I can't help but get caught up within these moments, harping on the impulsive desire to have you here in front of me *now*.

But then, I remember that time is gentle and all things that are truly meant to be will not pass me by; accepting that the timing of a journey is a museum of art and cannot be rushed.

COMPLACENCY

I feared her complacency; this sticky web of reasons she'd spun, melding her to the place she desired to be freed from- beholden to its consequences in tandem with keeping her wishes stretched thin amongst a tightrope cycling down under; a secret curiosity jutting from her heart, unable to keep its rhythmic longings at bay.

> *And if she could*, she'd chain her mouth and stitch her lips; threaded with her own heart strings plucked loose from the invisible twine tethering us as one- a far cry to uphold her fears to surrender to the feeling to let this ancient love bloom.

INFINITY IN POSSIBILITY

I want real.

I need raw,

aching for agonizing vulnerability

that would strip us bare in thoughts,

once too afraid to share.

I want truth. I need you,

less desirable to observe from beyond

a human touch,

shivering from cold hands

of a once remembered ghost.

I want reason.

I need proof;

to share in the existence

of a supraliminal connection-

the very thing they can't see,

but where infinity lies

within the possibility.

K. LA LUNE

A MOMENT WITH YOU

I'm encased in the ruins of a

kaleidoscope lens,

flushed with satin wishes and chaotic spurs of hope,

that hold dreams within these fingertips,

grasping your heart with hopeful eyes

that are only meant to dream of a moment spent with you.

READ AT 7:44 PM

Cause fuck, it just makes sense. *Us. We. You and I.* There's a lot of shit in this world that I'm unsure of, but knowing who owns my heart is probably the only thing I am sure of. I'm only whole when I'm with you and maybe that's my rambunctious heart talking. I can never silence its baying thuds when I think of you, or hear your name, or look at old photos. I can't be with anyone else without wishing to God it were you. Because, no one is you. No one could ever take your place, nor would I want them to try. Maybe, I'm in *way* over my head. It wouldn't be the first time and it won't be the last. Real love, as erratic and harebrained as it is, *should* drive you insane, make you question everything, only to come back to the same conclusion every time. Because, only then do you know it's "right." *And I know, it's you.* You are the only right in my life and I'm not ever, ever, ever letting that go.

K. LA LUNE

MESSY

I was messy,
but she was messier.
Scrambled minds splaying chaos
awaiting for all hell to break loose.
She's a rebel, I'm the recluse-
a duo of immeasurable strengths
and scattered brains;
power struggles and envy eyes,
caked with stars that shine
and tongues that weaponize
even the most beautiful of words;
devils in disguise.

IF THEY ONLY KNEW YOU

They say "*no one is perfect*," but that's not true- *they've never met you*, because if they did, they'd chew their words, pick at the crumbs between their teeth, only to spit them out and plea, "I'm sorry."

They'd see how the sun is your conduit; a force of ethereal thunder and lightning, striking magnetic poetry into the sockets of my eyes, while their rhythm rockets through every nerve ending attached to my body; how they pierce fire and ice, igniting a longing so agonizing, keeping me roped within the chase; hung by a chokehold of willowy dreams. Stunned in place, I'm lifted from my body, watching your heart widen with wonder each time that you smile.

They'd see how your body moves like golden seas, crashing a beautiful chaos at the base of my feet- and when your waves lull away, I'm fawning with the waters to take me down under, to drift afloat by the lullaby of all your unspoken words; a happily ever after.

HOW I MISSED YOU

Around you, these words stammer from their chambers, furling over clusters of tongue tied phrases; packages of love notes, strung together by satin tears from years-worth of missing you. These hands are clammy but you don't mind, slipping delicate fingers into the nooks of mine; a once mislaid piece now secure in its proper place- an intangible space that houses these ephemeral vitals keeping our soul alive.

I AM YOURS

For eight years, I've mouthed the words "*I am yours*" amidst the parallel on the wall- watching my lips blossom with a rosy flush, casting a portal of magic from the reflection.

I'd counted the days since we last spoke, preserving your voice and the way your eyes looked when staring into mine; reasoning with the lingering sense that fate was on our side- that something *extraordinarily peculiar* ran through our veins, trussing ourselves to each other's hearts, for now and for eternity.

For four years, I'd appealed with the sky, sealing pleas for your return, rattling off a million reasons why I needed you here and now.

They're always there; higher powers- listening, reminding me that no destiny can be altered or escaped; that *time is of the essence; be still and listen.*

I SHOULD HAVE KISSED YOU THAT NIGHT

I should have kissed you that night- when time aligned with the howling pulse of our hearts as your fingers brushed along my cheek, holding my entire lifeline in your eyes. It was that moment in which *I really knew*- when my heart leapt in wonderment, casting away any shrouded perplexity of the past, that I finally found you; awakened to our oath of eternal oneness.

I watched our mouths hang in limbo, parted slightly, barely touching- savoring in the familiarity of how long it's been since I've seen you.

Now, our radios have gone silent- comatose and frozen in time, waiting for the chosen hour to deliver fate back into our hands; a prophesized second, entwined with our blood from the time we were born and forever beyond.

K. LA LUNE

TURNING BACK TIME

If I could just hold onto the moment, let it fester, let it linger, let it grip this heart and smother it with all the time left in the world, *I would.*

I spent years pacing at the fold of this hope; that you'd appear from the far horizon, waiting for my touch; that somehow I'd be able to dance with your mirage, replenish what's starved with a spectral kiss.

I'd dreamt of the heavens moving mountains in lieu with the everchanging seasons of our past- the ways in which you left and never came back, while I walked amongst a tight line, gunning for your love.

A bystander, I'd applaud in quiet heaps of clamor- celebrate your wins from the wings, just happy to see you smiling.

If I had the kind of magic that poured time from my veins, I'd rewind every heartbeat, every breath, every dull-aching doubt, just to re-visit the day we parted ways; a moment that I was too afraid to say...

" I know you're the one"

BACK AGAIN

She's back again;

all five fingers gripped around my neck, pouring venom into my

mind, feeding it lies. I feel it- the warm blood surging through

my soul, keeping me roped within a cycle of loving her amidst a

void with no exit.

LIKE WAKING WITH THE SUN

to love her

is life

waking with the sun,

seeing heaven sculpt its magic, sparkling my eyes with wonder.

K. LA LUNE

BIRTHDAY CAKE

Every year, I still bake a cake on your birthday- blow out the candles, make a wish, and then fester in the ache. When it's late and the stars fail to sing me to sleep, I reason with the sky to send me a sign; that all is well in this journey of love- removing the confusion jutting wild from hungry eyes and weary bones.

IF ONLY YOU COULD SEE HOW BEAUTIFUL WE COULD BE

The dark pardons me from a day's torture, gifting me with tears of gold to nurse the ache that dwells where your name once stood. Your voice is woven within my thoughts, while memories of what never came to be sprout from the roots that connect the stars to my eyes; embedding our oath of destiny, sealing it with a kiss- a jagged dagger now grazing my lips with the undying virtue of a never-ending story; a book you were too quick to close, too afraid to re-open, and allow yourself to be loved.

If only you could see how beautiful we could be.

him

him | the man I promised to never love

WHAT A LIE, WHAT A LIE

"No, not now!" I thunder, slamming my frustration from mind to keyboard, attempting to blockade the growing currents of hindered visions convoluting around my eyes.

These time zones and state lines aren't enough to barricade the periling arousals that coagulate in summits of wishes at my feet. It's him that I want- undressed in his vulnerability, mouthing the words "I" and "love" and you", stringing them together loosely, convincing me completely.

It's when he lies to me that he hums a beautiful reverie; deep pocketed within these caves that echo a reverberation that blares over and over. I too, feed his lust, with an oath of loyalty, promising that it's "*only us*"; when really, that's not true.

In the forefront of my mind, she *waits* for me, to turn my attention back to center stage and claim the star that summons for my undying devotion.

SOUL ON FIRE

Caught in a landslide of vicious emotions, I'm tangled in his galvanizing embrace, clawing through barbed wire and quick sand pulling at the core of my heart space. One hand etched tightly amongst the divot in my spine and the other, tucked against my cheek, we sway to the melodious rhythms of the room around us burning down; fires of all that could be, left to fulminate and crash, crumbling the debris marked beneath the forbidden nature melting at our feet.

HOOK, LINE, AND SINKER

I don't know how,

but he's got me hooked.

reeled in by a wire clipped to my heart;
nothing but a crooked smile to capture me as bait.

WAKE ME UP WHEN THIS DREAM HAS ENDED

I'm staring into the mirror, catching my thoughts linger on the fixation of how I could be here with him. From behind me, he wraps his arms around my waist, pulls my milk chocolate hair and tucks it behind my ear, trailing kisses along the goosebumps on my neck. "*Good morning*," he breathes at the base of my ear, mapping his fingers towards the center of my chest, to my breast, and down to my stomach.

A euphoric sinking feeling bevels at my navel and I shift my eyes to his hands cupped around my belly. His gaze seems serene as he mirrors the same, caught in a whirlwind of "maybes" pouring in like rain; *to think that I could give him a child* one day. I sit with this rumination, allow it to absorb without judgement of what kind of mother I'd be.

Him? I know he'd make the perfect father (*if there ever was one*), even if he lacks the mental security to believe it himself; fears of upholding the essence of what the responsibility truly means. Still, there's a part of me that hopes that this isn't just a dream.

BEST KEPT SECRET

I'm his best kept secret. Only these four walls know what happens behind closed doors; when the blackening of the sky teems with tempt, initiating poison running untamed within these veins, conjuring chaos within. Claiming me as an extension of he, our mouths speak through aberrant movements, locked and loaded with intent to maim the fears that keep us running from the truth- our inseparability due to star crossed compatibility, simmering heavy angst that toil beneath our skin and route to our souls; activating regrets, a loss of control.

CUPID'S BOW AND ARROW

In a hazy twilight, he loves me raw- leaving nothing but bone; a listless protrusion of affection that keeps me on my toes, silently begging for more.

I'm lost amongst the blackened fires behind his stare that tell me *nothing.* Although afar, I can hear screaming from closed off stairwells leading to his heart- a basement padded with barbed wire deadbolts and caution tape plastered and strewn accordingly; keeping unwanted admittance from rearing its tantalizing sneer.

He's fallen in love- a quixotic paradigm barring logic from its grip, enveloping a man, once noncommitted, with the kind of extortion that'll leave him in the hands of Cupid's bow and arrow.

BREACH OF SECRETS

Midnight was made for him and i —

the breaking of day that danced away the saturation of the sky, clearing the canvas to paint more secrets that harbored between bones made of stone.

> There was a certain comfort about the darkened mass outstretched towards the vast city- suffused with notions of what "*they didn't know*,"; that I was his, submissive to the control of his hands wrapped around my jaw, bathing in an ocean of shadows claiming me behind hungry eyes.

I'd allow his temptations to devour me, relishing in the way he cupped my mouth and held my spine; how his fingers fit perfectly amongst the hollowed cavity trailing my backside.

From the French doors opened parallel to our dance of sin, the moon would watch with disapproving observation, but keeping our breach of lust a secret.

BRANCHES

I stare at the veins rising from your hand
like branches of a tree prodding from soul.
You grab hold of my face,
tracing the outline of my lips,
carefully and protectively.
My tongue glides along the salty surface,
tasting you before impeding to a dance of

entanglement

BLACK LACE

The tensions building as our destination seems to be drifting further away. You're transfixed by the way the California sun highlights my collarbone emerging from underneath my skin. Pulling my hair to the side, I glance over, watching your hands steel grip the wheel, tempted to wander elsewhere. You know exactly what I'm doing as you try to hide your smug demeanor, *but I know better.*

Hesitation sets in, resisting the urge to jeer your eyes off the road and onto my hand drawing the bottom of my dress up to my thighs. You're a sucker for black lace- the expensive kind you spend hours of the day fantasizing about. Beads of sweat trickle down the side of your face, giving away the lust you're defying. *But, I know you'll cave.*

The engine of your 69' Mustang erupts with heat as you push down on the pedal, hoping to release. Below your bottom lip, a droplet of blood hangs in limbo, punctured from the pressure of your teeth. You know I won't impede until you stop the car, feigning for a long-overdue dance of entanglement.

Little by little, I lift my dress just a bit more, and now you can see my blossom peak out from underneath the sheer black fabric. This time, you're unable to look away. The brown hues of your eyes turn darker as you wrestle with the tempestuous thoughts feeding your ego. *"Take them off,"* you growl, disturbance seething from your teeth.

K. LA LUNE

Naturally, I obey, slipping the nearly-nothing panties from around my hips, down to my ankles, and onto your lap. My scent drives you wild and I know it's vexing you as we continue on the 808, while the satin straps of my dress fall to my elbows.

Glancing over at your jeans, I gape at your growing anatomy. It's been far too long. "*Open your legs,*" you say with a firm yet calming tone. I please, submissive to your request. Your tongue glides across your lips, your eyes darkening once again, as the rest of you hardens.

Staring at soft porcelain skin, I can see the anguish protruding from your glare, wanting to dip your curiosity into the sweet abyss of "*it's been a long time coming.*"

Resilient you remain, until my hands hover over your boning mass, gripping you just as tightly as you grip the wheel. I'd forgotten how large you get when I'm around, fearing how tiny in comparison I am, but I know you fit *perfectly.*

It's not long until you begin to unravel- pent up anguish escaping from your body. With my lips pressed against your neck, I open my eyes, air ripped from my body as I see the delusions of my mistakes sitting in the back seat- her eyes punishing me with a mean stare.

ALL WE'LL NEVER BE

"I love the way you taste."

He's hungry for recipes of disaster- adamant about proclaiming me as his; a blood oath stained by the tip of our tongues, drawing forbidden ache from these bones carrying dense weight of all that we'll never be.

"RESPECTFULLY"

He rings me late at night- west coast burning on east coast dreaming; says he ain't asleep, but fantasizing about sex with me. Gruff voice, rambling off barely audible and brazen thoughts of all the things that keep him fixed on what drives him wild.

"*Respectfully*," he signs off with, lost in the windswept euphoria sweltered beneath heavy breathing. With him, I lose all sense of reality; romanticizing the mistakes I'll make under the influence of his illicit sayings- mesmerized in lieu with tantalizing sensations of sweaty bodies bonded together like glue, melding temptation with an afterglow resonance of one's lost grip of control.

TO BE LOVED

These actions run without consequence, breeding in a poison of one too many shots that now paralyze all rational thinking. I'm infinite while in the presence of hundred dollar champagne, choking on cigarette smoke stifling my lungs, while I'm sitting, legs wrapped around your backside on a billiards table; a private venue for you and your friends for the night- each time referring to me as your "girlfriend" when dropping love-bombed words in my honor.

I broke my promise, my streak, of not letting liquor fill these empty voids, but to permeate a mind as closed off and brash as his, I must level my conscious to meet his; to reach in and pickle with his fear of commitment- an exhilarating rush of curve balls, plot twists, and jump scares rounding each corner.

Somewhere deep, there's a soft spot for me- a peculiar red organ, baying shyly as it hides in the thrush, behind wrought iron fences and black smog; layers of barriers that wilt his desires to stay somewhere long enough.

Sigh.

That's all for one night, I decide, backing away from a heart that's just not ready to fully love or to be loved in return.

K. LA LUNE

THE PERFECT MAN ONCE EXISTED (I SAID ONCE)

Sometimes he'd just stare- a brooding darkness reeling in pools of black summits, fixating on controlling the temptation, yet indulging the wandering eye to bask in its beckoning affairs. Licking his lips from the adjacent couch, he gestures for me to slide over, sit on his lap, asking me to not allow his curious hands to touch a thing. Rules, they had to be drawn. We were addicted to the taste of forbidden fruit, obsessed with the chase that spun madly in every room. Of course, we never able to foster the agility to adhere to such things. Like magnets, we jolt from repellant to inseparable; mouths that sting with vigorous pleas and eyes that undress even the most poised; a despondent myriad of unrequited euphoria.

SUGAR PILL RUSH

As soon as the haze cleared from the overlook, sentiments procured within his words- illicit wonders pilling from their cage, once too reluctant to admit. Even in the moonlight, his eyes were the darkest shade of brown I'd ever seen- copious amounts of hardships buried deep within them.

Often, I'd crave the way his mouth turned upward when he watched me bite my lip, knowing I was feigning for his kiss, his touch, his scent- everything that lured me in. I was ruled by the dominant forbidden nature about us, addicted to the pure frenzy and sugar pill kind of rush it fed me.

I was in love with a man who could never commit to just one thing- *always* searching for the next big thing to call his own (for the time being). Admittedly, my sails sunk the day he told me I was trouble, alluding to the theory that he'd be unable to "quit me."

His polished sweet nothings haunt me within a dream state in which I'm tucked far away, unable to wake when the *visions becomes unholy.*

IS IT LOVE?

I'm a sucker for candlelit dinners and *he knows it*- grinning behind a napkin, I can already feel it. The room's moody veil of darkness leaves a trail of goosebumps along my skin, fidgeting with a noir of hauntingly beautiful disasters crawling between my hips.

Whether aware or not, he does this thing with his eyes and his lips; saying nothing but revealing everything behind a lustful brooding stare, holding escapism captive with thoughts that linger in mind- an enticement that often leads to an overdose of some kind; a regretful morning made from last night's mistakes.

It always comes knocking, *and I,* allow it back in. But tonight's different, I know it, as his energy shifts from cocky to tense; picking up on an unusual stutter and change in pitch in his voice.

"*What is it?*" I ask, wondering what could be keeping him perpetually edged.

"*You just look fuckin' perfect,*" he says, shaking his head while hiding the desire in his lap. Continuing, he admits, "*You're dangerous, you know that? No one does what you do to me.*"

"*You don't know how hard it's been to not fall in love with you,*" he resumes, ruminating on an eruption of feelings awaiting to implode within him.

Stunned, I choke on this resonance, feeling fluttery spasms hug my heart- a place that's only ever been touched by *her.*

RUN FOR THE HILLS

Lips locked and moving deviously, I'm pinned to the wall by a 6 foot something shadow. I'm submissive to his beckoning requests, unearthed from the inside out as he touches me in all the right places, wrong forbidden faces.

Time between our bi-coastal rendezvous' is both a punishment and a reward- siphoning desire over months of incredulous longing.

My body is his to wander and to implore beyond indefinable amounts. I'm the playground, center stage, the pearl in the oyster. To him, I'm Aphrodite- birthed from the sea, unhinged in all the best ways.

I forget reality exists when under his enigmatic charm, rushing through thresholds of fiery heavens and calming hells; cataclysmic forbiddances telling me to *run, run, run for the hills.*

BETTER LEFT UNSAID

"Could you ever see me the way you see her?" he asks, torn in vulnerability; a softness glazing over his eyes. The breeze howls around us, blaring the sting of truth deep into my ears.

For a moment, I'm lost in my own clamoring thoughts, jailed behind an angst that cooks angrily under pressure. My tongue's been mislaid in the clouds; only speaking with the tang of unconditioned love for the one whom no one could ever replace.

And, he knows;

he knows that this love is sewn with a myriad of lifetimes- each stitch awash in golden prophecy, kissed by the constellations and all of its apprentices; an anomaly that one could only dare to dream.

My silence is loud enough to pierce daggers and stir flames, obliterating a heart that's been fooled by the lonely touch of someone who aches for another heart.

I cast my reserve as I look beyond the horizon, allowing the moment to pass, hoping it would translate better if I leave all these things unsaid.

CHEERS TO NO WILLPOWER

A dinner… to talk… as nothing more than 'just friends'; I'm rolling in skepticism as his voice beckons me from the other end. A knock at the hotel room door sounds and a courier is outside with a ribbon-wrapped box perched amongst both arms.

"*For you, Ms. Lune,*" he's gentle and I'm sighing, reluctant to open what I already know awaits inside. Of course… agent provocateur in my size, black and lace, and just his type. But that's not all. A satin dress is tucked beneath with a price tag of four month's rent.

"*Before you call to cancel, I'm not going to touch you… unless you consent-*" a handwritten note condemns. It's almost 9 PM and I've sat naked on this couch, fidgeting with the idea of going or staying. I can smell his cologne wafting from the box, burying me deeper into a sinful night of living.

He loves me in black- it vexes him wildly, pulling the devil himself from the coves of a wilted heart; a darkened space where I'm hypnotized, summoned by the blackened pinnacles of hunger calling me by name. *Fuck.* I'm dressed and I look like something he won't be able to resist. I'm backing away and yet my feet keep drifting down the hall and into the escalade that he's sent for me.

Champagne and strawberries await inside- so cliché but proper; a rich man's minimal gesture. It should be noted that dinner for us is not what you may think. It's pleasure and play, and I'm the food- a most decadent treat.

CHEERS TO NO WILLPOWER PT II

On the drive to the Hollywood Hills, I fuss with the stitching of this dress- thousands of dollars; his hourly pay for the simplicity of existing. "*See you soon*," my phone buzzes; his name alone summoning pleasure as I shift my bearings in the back seat of the escalade.

It's been twenty-five minutes and I've ran through a list of reasons to back away now. For one, he holds too much power- keeping me pried open to water these flowers, sprinkle them with a blackened tonic; a syphoning stupor pouring ink into these roots, where it spreads through my veins, creating an addiction that his absence can't replace.

Two: he's wrong for me in all the obvious ways- when he sends outsized bouquets, signing the card with a fake name- a quirky one liner to keep me stained of his memory.

And lastly, he could *never* be mine- no wonder I've fallen under-spellbound from the aftertaste of what I'm forbidden to keep- a transfixing buzz that will only garner the desire to come back for more.

When I arrive, he's outside in a black suit and tie, two champagne flutes balanced in both hands. I'm greeted by his ultra-rich dark eyes, a kiss on the cheek, quieting the hunger inside.

WOMAN IN DENIAL

The office smells of floral, clouded in the stench of all I've been avoiding. The women, they're unhinged, gathered like an occult and tabled around my desk.

"*It's for you*," they chant, evasive in silent chatter.

A copious bouquet is on display, covering the surface of my work station- a sneaky metaphor for a wandering mind, sculpted by a man whose riches make me upheave in guilt, shadowing what's real.

"*It's too easy to fall in love with you. I hope these make you smile as much as you make me do*,"- the card reads, positioned intently amidst the center of 4 dozen flowers.

I should call and say thank you, but I know what'll follow; a private jet, some French caviar, and a one way ticket to the piteous downfall of a *woman in denial*.

pages to tattoo memories of others

pages to tattoo memories of others | the seasons and reasons

WITH ANOTHER

I'm alone with my focus fixed on the ceiling, stirring the pot inside of my head, boiling over with lurid praises that shower my pride. As my eyes roll back into my head, I know that you have another women in your bed, yet with her, you're unraveling in thoughts of me and all of the nagging lust I've left between your legs.

A roaring smirk smears across my face, raising these cheekbones high towards the sky; it's when I think of your mouth linked with hers, revered that I'm still stained fresh on your tongue as her lips meet yours; she can taste me and her mind starts to fetter.

She's now hindered by my ghost coasting deep behind your eyes, understanding that you're some place different, in a world untouched by her hands- an arsenal of wonder where I carve moonlight into your bones, stretching your soul, laying it out like a sea of dandelions in an open field.

Does she know that you're the sun and I'm the moon?- that when our hearts touch and our breathing hastens, we embody the epitome of the holy divine spirit?

She must know that you're a woman of a plethora of dreams, yet *somehow you still only crave me.*

CAMI

Curiously, I'd acquired a sweet liking to the waitress,

losing myself in a dangerous daydream,

where I'd whisk her away,

allowing my lips to wander along her neck

as I'd plead my case,

wanting to be more than friends.

While writing down my order on a piece of paper,

[stolen from the notepad in her back pocket,]

she'd bite her lip.

"Kiss me," I'd write.

Initially, she'd tease until I'd lift her,

placing her on the sink,

where she'd wrap her legs around my waist.

Snap out of it, back to reality-

her eyes had locked with mine

and I'd wondered if she was a mind reader

as she kept her gaze firm-

a shy smirk growing amongst her face,

her eyes shifting ever-so-often from my eyes to my mouth

to the lace of my bra peeking out.

For a split moment,

my unrequited heroine didn't exist

as my impulsive heart throbbed

for the mystery girl walking past.

Never keen on dirty blondes but a sucker for green eyes,

my stare followed her as she made her way

to the table in the back corner of the bar,

where she'd keep checking over her shoulder from time to time.

K. LA LUNE

She's flirting,

I think.

Making her way back over, she hands me the bill

Dismissive to the amount,

I narrow in on her name on the top right

Camille.

WORLD'S APART

I want to explore every unknown ruin mapped inside of you- every icy mountain, molten center, charismatic anomaly. I want to feel the budding of your curves, your breasts tracing along the base of my fingers, merging through the cracks. I want to taste every scar that's made you, *you*. I want to catch a glimpse of your mind, study its brilliance, allowing your veins to stain my eyes with the colors of your soul- bridging the gap between our ages, our cultures, our worlds. I want to feel the rush in the chase, tempted by the things I can't grasp between my fists. I want to read you, inside and out, devouring plot twists and loopholes; stitch myself to your pages until I've absorbed it all. I want to make you feel as infinite as you make me believe; feed the noir of uncertainty keeping me in place, trussed to your magnetic metaphorical embrace.

VERONICA

To find yourself within the reign of Veronica is an experience like none other. Some are able to tolerate the harsh environment and others are gone before they've even taken off their coats.

She's conventionally beautiful- porcelain skin with silky hair as dark as a raven's feathers. Above her top lip, to the right, a faint scar's left behind from a fistfight she won in middle school (it's her go-to ice breaker story).

Like a vampire, her eyes change color from brown to green to devilishly yellow when she's angry- which is more times than not. She's cocky but it's deserved, working as hard as most people I know.

One time, I visited her family home in Jersey, where the walls of her childhood bedroom were a deep violet underneath all the miscellaneous magazine clippings. From the time she was six, she knew she wanted to be a magazine editor and work for the biggest company in New York City. Twenty-one years and a graduate degree later, that's exactly where she found herself. When Veronica wants something, she gets it- *simple.*

Upon meeting her, you might want to run- her personality is not everyone's cup of earl grey tea in the morning. Her brutal honesty would hail splinters of glass, piercing anyone's confidence. But, it's what I admire most about her because with Ronnie, *nothing* is sugar- coated.

Wearing sky-high red bottoms and perfectly tailored suits during business hours, she shifts her persona, easily. But come nighttime, she's in her sweats, pouring tequila shots, demanding we chug or "be a little bitch." Life's a little bit sweeter with a tiny pinch of salt.

There are, of course, a lot of great facets under the surface once you scrape off the callous pieces. Loyal to a fault, she's like a safe. Any secret you tell her is locked away, for good, no matter who you are. If someone is bothering you, forget it, they're toast. Without hesitation, she'll go to war for you and fight battles and win arguments like she's in the courtroom.

And yet, she's not as scary as she initially seems. Quick to her defenses, she'll never admit it, but secretly, she's sensitive. If you're ever able to crack her open, there's tumultuous molten lava oozing at the core, but it's hard to break that shell.

If you ever find yourself witnessing her shed a tear, consider yourself four-leaf-clover lucky. It means she really likes you.

NO PLACE LIKE HERE

"*This one's different, I can feel it,*" I reason, telling my pesky logic to take a back seat. My heart is aware of the bruising it'll take, placing its delicate pulse in the hands of a woman who only has eyes for someone who isn't me.

But, my God… *the chase-* it powers every last drop of sanity fueling the fires burning fast.

It rallies from the sidelines with a shameless sneer, cycling like a cyclone roaring caution against the wind.

She's placed me under her enigmatic spell; charmed by the recipe of a foreboding disaster. But, I'm wide-eyed and mislaid beneath her olive skin; heavy lust hammocked between reality and foolery;

a place I've come to know a little too well.

GOLDEN VOICE

Head full of thoughts, I run to my typewriter, purging the venomous heart throbbing's that stick to my guts like tiny seeds. The page becomes bruised with all the messy-unkept admittance's pooling around these words- words I've never even heard, but hold and understand because *you're them*; every intricate and carefully crafted letter binding your essence, beautifying phrases.

They come to me by travel of your voice; like inconsistent tides, a staccato skipping beats- a unique rhythm putting a showman in his place.

The ink is black but once absorbed onto paper, it's gold; riddling me with more curiosity than before.

THE COOLEST GIRL

Without warning, it found me- that provoking void, summoning intangible contradiction somewhere deep inside. A jarring-exultant rush, seamlessly laced with a fleeting array of colors.

Tempestuous thoughts, unraveling faster than the speed of light, coated the so-called "norm" of my identity, beckoning an emergence within.

Dry lumps formed in my throat, choked up when she'd walk on by as my shaky fingers gathered beads of sweat within its clenched fists. I swallowed hard, biting my lower lip- the faint taste of a blood droplet staining my tongue, clueing me in on what was befalling.

She had an attitude- a witty and confident boast about her. I'd pledge it was enough to make me fall to my knees, gushing at the seams.

With curiosity, my sight would wander to her lips as she'd speak, and visions of my mouth pressed against hers would taunt me for the entirety of our shift. *Still, I felt like the coolest girl.*

The warm summer-night air heated my ego as I walked to the passenger side of her car, head held high, rallying the inner demon clawing at the surface to escape.

Quietly, I'd shush her, wanting to savor the moment for as long as I could until the night would end, and reluctantly, I'd turn back into a pumpkin. For now, I was her right-hand jester, and I wouldn't have changed a thing.

Between the elated emersion of pure euphoria, the wind blowing my hair, and the reverberations of "The Show Must Go On," filling the car, *I definitely felt like the coolest girl.*

I'd forgotten how short the car ride was, feeling my spirits drop, not wanting the moment to end as we approached the house where our small get-together would commence.

Alas, we made it.

Through my boozy delusional fog and lurid expressions, I took a leap of faith, shutting the bathroom door so tightly that only my morning regrets could be heard, voicing their violent fists against the wood.

The moment blinked quietly as soft lips brushed over mine, morphing drunken actions into sober realities. Unprepared for the long road ahead, I now knew a single moment could change everything.

And although the memory was stolen away too quickly by the inexorable workings of time, there will forever be that one sentiment embellished upon my youth- *that I'll always feel like the coolest girl.*

K. LA LUNE

IN THE FINE PRINT

Somewhere in the fine print,

I must have signed away my heart to the unrequited touch of all those whom I would never have.

K. LA LUNE

CREATURE OF THE NIGHT

Head slamming against the floor, I do not wish to harm myself, yet I yearn to set my heart free of this burden; to knock and jolt this wild spirit, whose giddy eyes seek adventure in the cruelest conditions- chasing violet streams of euphoric musings, sprinklings of love dust in each breath of an unrequited delusion. A creature of the night, I'm love-bombed and in love with the infatuation of what I can't have; mercilessly obsessed with the thickening of blood that flushes through my heart, warning me of an overdose setting sail along the ebbs and flow of these hauntingly beautiful shadows- the ones who sink their prolific snares deep into the parts of me that leave me bare; stripped down to fingernails that claw for one more moment before reality snatches me from the grips of my imagination.

INVITATION TO HEARTACHE

I harvest the cruelest intentions when it comes to affairs of *my* heart- carefully crafting their strings, stitching them together like golden twine under a midnight sky. Easily severed, I leave them loose, knowing that when they snap and the pain begins to render, I'll be carved from the inside out, spiraling amongst the harshest emotions that'll rattle me raw; an exalt of chaos blooming beautifully from these shallows.

Heartache is neither

black nor white,

it's both the sun and the dark side of the moon.

I sculpt these harebrained words fluttering from my chest, molding them to extract the essence of a heart worth breaking, over and over again- a masochistic hunger beckoning to insatiate a gamut of periling unknowns.

EVERYTHING

She's everything I'm not; *everything* I wish to be; *everything* I wish to hold in my hands- allowing the desires to pool within the crevices of skin that trace from my heart to hers.

LIKE THE MOVIES

It's late and I'm her shoulder to lean on. *Divorce…* don't know anything about it, but pretending I do for the sake of appearing helpful.

While she's barreling through years of trauma, I'm lost in the ever glow of these city lights, remembering my own landslide of mistakes, kicking myself straight in the gut… *metaphorically, of course.*

"You write so beautifully," she sniffles, wiping away a droplet of a tear sitting softly on her cheek.

"I only write so beautifully because *she* makes it so easy," I admit, letting her know that there's only ever been 'one.'

"She's lucky," she admits, sliding her hand gently into my left jean pocket, finding my fingers that are clammy from her presence. She continues once she's peaked my attention, "I've always wondered what it'd feel like… *kissing another woman.*"

Alert and doe-eyed, I'm dazzled in a flash of my own inability to feign in curiosity. I've thought about her before; now curbing my own late night desire to remain respectful.

But, it's too late… my blood is rushing winding rivers of lust, saturating every hypothetical daydream with what might happen next..

Her mouth smells of citrus and mint and I'm intrigued, inching my lips closer to hers, to feel her breath warm my face.

"Are you sure?" I ask, preparing for a taste.

OURS

It's late while I swim under the velvet sky, wandering the streets that hold her name. With each step, another piece of the story unfolds, running in tandem with a heart full of nostalgia through my blood still awash with memories.

I'm lost in a fictitious fog, riding autopilot in the direction of a star struck string of fate, listening to the caroling of voices leading me towards paradise.

I'm half asleep with no cognition of where I'm heading- only bewitched by the chasms of all that's meant to be. I arrive at a hotel close by, unable to carry these bones further.

My eyes trail the skyline, gut punched by the sinking pool of lead weighing me down like a sandbag under gravity's magnetic kiss of death.

It's *the hotel*- a place embossed with her initials, our destiny; a universe of its own, standing tall in the heart of all that once was.

Chilled by the turn of events, I mellow to an even keel, nursing a floodgate of tears from crashing storms in the midst of a lobby full of strangers.

"Whatever room you have available," I mutter, peeling the tang of bitter whiskey away from my lips.

I'm handed a room key and ushered to the 9th floor, lobbied to stare fortune in its gleeful eyes; *the room.*

Once inside, I succumb to the ground, feeling her presence rooted around the space, prodding me from behind the walls- a rosy flush returning from the diluted shade of pewter and alabaster across my cheeks.

I'm wrapped in a limbo-bonded storm of emotions, curving dodges of feelings that now spindle around my vertebrae.

"If only you were here," a gentle plea escapes, knowing that from even state lines away, her heart is only a whispered call away.

MORTAR AND PESTLE

She grinds what's left of me like a mortar and pestle, stealing life from each hidden nook inside this cavernous pit. I'm charmed by her wit, folding at the mere mention of her name, plumaged by the way she says mine. I can sew this bruised and tattered heart back with the ever glow of her voice- floating along the octaves that kiss me to sleep.

FORK IN THE ROAD

I'm hesitant to feed my honesty- feelings I've buried, words that have pitted me against myself; that *you* ... may never choose me.

> *I don't want to be a choice-* as though I'm one path jeered from a fork in the road;

> a piteous beckon calling for your attention, surmising in cavernous shadows while I summon for more hope to find me-

> holding this invisible string of fate taut like a lifeline, a parallel life source, connecting me to you.

UNCHARTERED TERRITORY

You loom above me,

hovering with intent

as I'm tempted to

look up.

My pulse hastens

and I wonder

if you're

able to hear the

thudding clamor

banging at my chest.

I sneak a peek,

careful not to seem

too allured

by the satin-smooth

skin along the nape

of your neck.

Swallowing hard,

my heart rate accelerates

with an impending climax,

watching you watch

me, wondering

if you too, are curious.

K. LA LUNE

SUCCUBI

Midnight awakens; leaving a trail of your memory. I'm displaced within a chaotic dream state, pinned down by an unknown force whose control feigns to see the life drain from my eyes, fed by an ache of desire boiling within my blood.

But, I'm not scared.

In fact, I entice this creature to enter, take what's mine in exchange for her secrets. As she obliges, I'm roped within these illicit visions- harebrained scenes of her and I entwined in a hypnotic and intimate dance of entanglement.

> *Sex with a demon*; a version of herself stuck in the closets of her subconscious- an illusion she feeds when a man rejects her gift to love and be loved in return.

We lock eyes and it's then in which she realizes that I'm not like the others who only swim to sink, but that I love her unconditionally, *devotedly*.

a chatty mind and a wordy tongue

a chatty mind and a wordy tongue | not everyone's cup of fucking tea

HEED THE CRY OF THE LONE WOLF

Peel back the layers of a lone wolf and unearth a legacy of broken dreams perpetuating stillness underneath; bones of those who carry the weight of a million reasons why the bitter tang of a journey can change the trajectory of how one perceives life to be.

Fallen across the crescent moon, she howls for the stars to sparkle her gold, to cascade in droves of midnight magic, filling hollow nooks with mystical interludes- a rhythm to pacify a weary heart turned silent from arduous attempts to keep it tethered to a chokehold held taut; by time slipping in and out of a merciless drought.

AN ISLE IN THE STORM

I'm far away from where I once stood; on an island without sun. The coastal breeze off the shore of these mysterious seas carry hymns of all the lost promises you failed to keep; letters that faltered and fell to the depths, now sunken and drenched in misfortunate regrets. I'm restless as I reason with the waves that crash along my feet. They're as angry as the monsters who berate my mistakes, forcing me to live and re-live those blunder-struck moments, keeping me stuck in the sinking pits of oblivion as I welter with the unapologetic passing of time slipping through my fingertips. But, I'm stunned in place as daylight breaks and the tides cease, lulling over the divots of a once unpromising dread. An eclipse rolls over the eastern sky, bestowing me a second chance to take back what's mine.

.

WATERED WITH POISON

Incredulously, my mind doesn't allow me much time to float alongside the sapphire skies, bursting with delicate visions of your sunny eyes once fixed upon mine. While picking daisies from the gardens that sprout from the soil, tiny prickling's of unease draw disseminating apprehension, staining the once alluring meadows, now tainted with visceral poison.

BREADCRUMBS

I'm lost in the fleeting arousing's that hold me in a love-stricken overdose, hungry to feel more of what you've bread-crumbed me with;

lies and endless wonder.

TROPE OF FEAR

For so long, I'd been tainted by the pulsing echoes of meaningless hearsay- lost and sodden amidst wallowing trenches; a victim to an unknown revolution, soldiering alongside ploys that'd set my soul on fire, leaving me tattered and weathered in a pool of my own blood, my own implemented conundrums. But the remedy always coasted effortlessly within, just waiting for me to realize the potential waiting to emerge beyond this hollowed trope of fear.

BEHIND THE CRACKS

The mirror has become a stranger too

> a soulless reflection lost behind a withered shell, gone
> with the years that fell away too soon; a porcelain face,
> now hardened by a brash aftertaste that lies dormant
> at the fold of these cracks.

The pieces, they chip- mistakes gutting like vines from the
depths, shrinking and curling dreadful roots around my eyes;
tying me to these idealities that devour me come night.

MILK OF AMNESIA

Heavy lids losing give to a milky gravity, I'm tunneling under. The lights begin to blur, all these faces multiplying in droves, but my focal lens remains fixed on one set of eyes. No, I don't try to fight it, but I'm poetically driven by the escapism feigning beneath my pulse; losing mobility to speak or move on my own. One second feels like ten, and she's still holding my hand. I will myself to stay lucid in the moment, holding onto stars rocketing from her chest, leading me down into an induced sleep- a beguiling void of blackness, a block of time that sits idle in my mind; the closest delirium to the bitter tang of "nothing."

GOING UNDER

A familiar touch and I'm sinking- falling into the receding airwaves pulling me away from reality. She's there, holding my hand, grasping my soul as I'm led into hollowed darkness, inept and without control. Blurring details lull me away, yet I'm fixed on her eyes as they watch me drift.. *further, deeper, heavier* until I'm under; amiss within a void, awaiting to be woken by the sonorous respite of her voice.

RHYME WITHOUT REASON

I'm stuck in this rhyme without reason- bitten by perplexing sweet nothings embrocating along my skin like a velveteen feather lost in the wind. Turning a blurred eye towards the foreboding reality, I'm one hop down a narrowing rabbit hole, catching hopeful glimpses of all that'll never fortify outside of the redolent sunbeams that dance in between my eyes. I'm the main attraction of a daunting metaphor; to always chase what I'm reluctant to grip within the smalls of my fingers- and yet, I still simmer in the beauty of each emotion that comes along with it.

TO THE STARS

Pinned down by percussive blaring's of all that I'm reluctant to accept, I fight with the lyrical antagonists that battle with this stubborn view that I have of you- a gamble and midnight game of dirty roulette, placing bets on fate and the timing and workings of when it'll all take place; signs indoctrinating my mind, feeding it whimsical musings that I open at the folding of daylight when the sky meets the indigo-bruised face of dusk, reeling me onward to sit with the stars, confessing an extravagant panoply of affection with bundles of love notes tied up by these heart strings, plucked loose as each day passes without you.

NAKED

Quieted by the mysterious hums within the vast anomaly of the universe, I'm urged to strip bare, unveil my spirit- as naked as the skin caging my heart; peel away the caked layers covered in old wise tales- no longer suited for the places I'm destined to reach; an ineffable landscape of beautifully violent dreams- growling changes thundering through the book of my soul, restoring life upon the once devoid pages of hope.

THINNING OF THE VEIL

These eyes house lyrical reveries full of letters that speak of her phases; the way she sways in a syzygy with the moon and its changes- leaving just as quickly as these dreams that drain from my fingers; ink stained scars that bleed within the penumbra of all hope that's been lost- misplaced amongst a labyrinthine plot twist, as thick as the veil that shrouds me with doubt.

WHAT'S MINE

Out my window, the sky would seize; purple bruises birthing neon hues as I buried the strife of losing you to another. The clouds drifted in tandem with my thoughts, carrying visions of all that's been lost- a war in which I'd surrendered, bargaining with a higher power to show me what's mine amidst a gamut of uncertainty and infamous callous misunderstandings.

I KNOW LOVE!

Love promises that she'll find me when I've ditched my armor and tore away my dubious blunders of doubt. But, *those thoughts*, they crawl like tiny ants, sticking to each and every baby hair trailed amongst my body. I wipe away the ick, moving my body in sways of disgust.

Love looks at me and laughs as I dance away the intrusive barrels of "buts," takes me by the hand, offering a taste of her nurturing touch, her cosmic medicine. It's familiar and warm, and I succumb to its perplexing waft of remembrance.

I know Love! She's with me every night, in the shape of my heart and the one who's soul is the other half of my own. She's the faceless oddity that wraps me tightly, cushioning soft kisses amongst the scabs that itch to burst wide open again.

Love *is* me- she's timeless, unconditioned to the unforgiving nature of life's cruelest beatings.

THE CAGED BIRD WILL SING

Synonymous with a caged bird, whose wings are tied in electric twine, I'm distastefully swaddled within chaos' grip. When I open my mouth to speak, I begin to choke as the words ricochet from the backside of my teeth, falling towards the abyss from where they once came-

> sizzling anger in fiery infernos down under, toiling with angst as more time passes, and I'm still stuck here waiting; waiting with more poetic psalms to appease your flare for melodramatic affairs- Romeo and Juliet pirouetting through a burning castle beside a summit on the hill.

These letters, they decay while my fingers bruise with age, and I'm anointed in the thick dew of your honey-bombed charm; wilting at the seams, praying for this release.

TO THE SKY

Scatterings of mist off the sea, I'm enveloped in the California coastal breeze, immersed in the suns hypnotic rays of infinite possibilities. Below me is the pier and I must be 20 feet from its deck, but I ache to reach higher into the clouds, where I'm bathed in moonlit petals and incandescent shadows. I wish to reach beyond the moon and its silver lakes, beyond the constellations that carry my fate. I wish to soar and rocket through space, seeking comfort in all of life's riddles, while coddling my woes in the embrace of a higher power.

FINDING THE RELEASE

It is the thunder who empathizes with my rage, summoning ashy clouds from caves in the sky. I bellow with anger, shout the most vile rhymes knotted at the core where light was once driven. Menacing snarls of apocalyptic booms scourge in the distance, piercing the space above my head with a fuse-lit clamor, matching the putrescent words that spit fire from the depths; retrusion of my teeth while these librettos splice and tear through my mouth, ripping open my pinkish tongue within its hellish release, leaving the blood to pool at my feet.

BLACK LILITH

Idle in the midst of these blooming fields, I'm rooted to the soils from the inside of my chest; lucid in wild wonders of stupor filling these once hollowed voids.

Come quarter past midnight, when the indigo velvet skies devour me in moon fall, I'm swept away by the ache you bare in song, calling for me from faraway lands, to hold and to cherish the unseen moments in time;

an escape to lift the veil beyond the divide that claims to separate you and I- *but only for so long* can the black Lilith suppress what's destined to have been foreseen, for when the heavens rain and sing their praise, there's no stopping two hearts meant to be.

AFTER THE NIGHT CEASES FIRE

Poetic agony dawns on me come morning as I'm lifted from the clouds, moon fall still fresh on my fingertips. Sunshine fills these heavy eyes and I'm covered in the thick dew of our dreams, perforated by your midnight departed absence. A wave of ache devours me quickly, while my soul is still lingering amongst the skies that hold me as I descend back to reality. I swallow the burn of your embrace, lost somewhere in a void that I can no longer taste, breathing cries of loss, having

HOW CRUEL THE DARK CAN BE

God only knows how cruel the dark can be, observing my heart decay within the lone grips of losing you. Displaced in angst, I built a fortress out of misery; drinking this elixir in hopes to rewind the moments that have fell through my fingertips, flooding regret in a lake of tears.

Inside of my mind, your voice laps as I swim in all of its octaves, coasting ashore at the fold of its echo rippling beneath me. I move with the chatter of the clock on the wall, waiting for the perfect moment to find me in its ominous stillness; to warn me of the dagger disguised as hope, making a home for itself amidst the curving of my spine; hungry for my pleas; devouring them entirely.

HOW I'D LOOK IN WHITE

Caught amongst the incandescent glisten of my reflection in the mirror, I'm eyeful in wonder; twirling every which way, speculating how I'd look in white- how the delicate tendrils of my hair would fall amongst my face, nimble in a cascadic draping; hiding my evermore blush at the sight of you gawking across from me and down the aisle. The room becomes our center stage- a union of soul, a merging of the sun and the moon as one; where upon the beat of a bewildering staccato, I'd vow to love you through every life, through every wayward upheaval that'll attempt to keep us apart.

K. LA LUNE

FAMILIAR STRANGER

With him, I'm unclothed from my soul's armor; an almost stranger, whose mouth beckons forth a lyrical reverie of familiarity- a voice that breathes spiritual sonnets beneath my skin, perpetuating chaos at the fold of a stillness. Shyly, I'm flushed with innocent ache; a harebrained desire to feel his touch caress what dwells amongst a moonlit trance- a cataclysmic resonance, comprised of fiery vowels that escape from his lips and wander towards translation of what hides between my hips; a fine-tuned crescendo building in tandem with the way my heart skips its beats; my fingernails digging imaginative treasures into the abyss of these sheets.

kiss from the poet

kiss from the poet | chef's special

MY GHOST

My ghost walks beside me,

haunting me,

ripping at the masterpiece

that I've created.

She says,

"no happiness for you, my dear."

In an instant,

she's gone, and I'm left

with a regretful-binding decision.

It leaves me paralyzed

every single time.

When I look for my ghost,

she's nowhere to be found.

She's nothing but a visual façade-

a fabrication of my disillusioned reality;

a daunting metaphor

for my unusual expectations.

My ghost once said to me,

"You're going to hell, my dear."

She's only there

when I wish she weren't,

hiding underneath the layers of doubt,

seeping through the

cracks of my mistakes-

K. LA LUNE

that's where she plays;

reminding me of my past,

while relentlessly chaining me

to the hell of my fears.

When I breathe,

she steals the air from my lungs

and says,

"You don't need that, my dear."

I suffocate at the mercy of my ghost-

the one who walks beside me,

haunting me,

tormenting me-

binding me to the places

from which I once escaped.

She lures me in-

my ghost, she knocks

She says,

"may I come in, my dear?"

Each time her small fists

pound against the wood,

I shudder, but regretfully,

I open the door.

"You're here to kill me, aren't you?" I ask.

Flawlessly resilient,

she snickers, "only if you let me."

K. LA LUNE

I back away from the mirrored image,

frightened that my end is near.

She says, "Don't be afraid, it's just little old me."

Proceeding with caution,

I command her to leave

and never return.

"If you want me gone,

then why did you let me in, my dear?"

The answer is so cumbersome,

led by a heavy release.

I close my eyes

and shout, "you can't hurt me."

And, vanished,

my ghost, she's gone,

and now I'm freed.

CATHARSIS

Pragmatic.

I'm filled with a curiosity for wonderment. Delving into cavernous topics, I bide my time between logic and emotion. Often, the two buckle under, combatting loudly in the nooks of my mind, rebutting one another with fair points. I spend the majority of my days thinking about *everything.* Over time, I've acquired a specific skillset that allows me to separate the two, only using one or the other as needed. Almost-always, I lead with my heart, letting my mind take the backseat, while I cry and fill my diary with romantic tragedies- a catharsis to understanding where it begins and deciding where it ends.

THE COFFEE DATE

Displaced somewhere in the rear of the café,

coffee beans grind as crowds fill the line,

and I watch with cautious eyes.

I peer around, looking for that someone,

but I know they aren't showing.

So, I sip my latte,

tapping my index finger on the table,

hoping to draw attention away from my

wandering eyes in fears I may seem lonely.

when the hell did i become so needy?

Caring what other people think of me…

I've developed this paranoia within me

and at times I can't quiet the noise it makes-

disrupting my one-woman coffee date.

K. LA LUNE

So, I begin to conversate with the voice in my head

as we go through the ebbs of success,

quickly changing the subject-

noticing how dark the interior is.

How the trumpets from the speakers

fill each ear canal with wandering thoughts,

sparks of creativity-

they crash down, unexpectedly,

like waves from the tides waking me up.

I reach for a napkin

and search for a pen,

beginning to write again-

starting with the first line.

So predictable,

so cliché.

A poet...

displaced somewhere in the rear of the café.

K. LA LUNE

132

TRAIN CAR # 744

It was peculiar, I'll admit, gliding along the rusted tracks as the sun danced through the space. *Assumingly*, I was being haunted by a clandestine sequence.

With each fleeting emotion, it found me, signaling an awakening of sorts- a truth I'd discover in just a few years.

> *Train car number 7444 kept me warm when my soul was not a home.*

Even if only for sixty-four minutes, its aura found and enveloped me with hope- the kind in which only true miracles were kept locked away and safe from human hands. Only those who believed could see and for some reason, that person was *me*.

I'd spent a lot of time alone on that train, always sliding into the same seat on the left- the beginning of a serendipitous tradition.

On late nights, while heading home from my ventures in the city, I'd leave defeated, wanting to escape the void that always latched onto me.

Too drunk to pay attention, too sad to notice my surroundings, I'd take my seat and shroud my face from those who passed by, embarrassed by my vulnerable side.

Looking up, I'd gasp when I finally take notice of the large 7444 etched atop the left corner of the train. Almost instantaneously, I'd fall asleep and forget my worries, knowing I was protected for another sixty-four minutes.

K. LA LUNE

133

Some days, train car number 7444 would not arrive and I'd slump down the aisle, and situate myself to a seat on the right. After all, I was along for the ride, preoccupied by the noise of my thoughts combatting loud within.

Memories of her would turn happy times into physical ache. I'd well up quickly, viewing her through blurry tears before they'd drop to my lap, and *she'd again*, disappear.

When the train would come to a halt at the connecting station, I'd watch passengers exit and enter simultaneously.

Intuitively, as though something were calling my name, I'd move my eyes to the left and that's when I'd see train car number 7444 sitting parallel to my gaze on the adjacent track.

A powerful release of exhaust, bellowing from its mighty mass, had reminded me *that all is well.*

This became our thing.

I'd ride the railroad for many more days through many more years and train car number 7444 would always be there to greet me, to be reminiscent with me on the journey I'd embarked upon- a prelude of what would come in the years to follow, to always remember the magical feat in knowing that *I'm never alone.*

CRACKS OF THE MOON

Nightfall seeks what here shall miss. The air burns my lungs as I breathe deep, inhaling all the false hope clinging to the atmosphere. I chase danger and watch my sanity peel away slowly as I run to the edge, tempted to jump.

The tears rush and plummet, the floodgates opening wide, heartache seeping into the cracks of my mistakes. But, I float on your high, blissfully reminiscent.

Drunk as I may be, the lucidity of my heart navigates its way to the corner of eighty-fifth and Lexington, where my fingers trace along the faded ink on the brick wall- our initials and a sonnet reciting our story.

One with the city streets, midnight looms over our faces, illuminating your crimson cheeks stung from the chilling winds. "*Let's run away*," you say with a wicked smile. I search for that voice, following it until it leads me home.

Reluctantly, I accept. I stand alone outside this hotel room- desolate, cold, and entirely ours.

Shadows rage along the walls, casting a silhouette of our younger days. The room spins but I remain fixed in one spot, admiring the intimacy of our once upon a time.

K. LA LUNE

We're two halves of the same flame, fearing only what the mind dictates, what it feeds off of, what it does to dissolve the memories.

Our strength is tested as isolation and distance play mind tricks on us, perpetually keeping us doubting the power of fate.

I'm marked by times scars- by the very thing that fuels the longing enclosed around my heart. Painfully, at times, I wish we'd never met; that I'd never fallen in love with the one thing that could destroy me, but I don't really mean that.

I'll fill hollow voids with exultant times, remembering the life before the awakening that swept you away. I'll hang onto any last fragment of what you left behind and vow to treasure those feelings till death do us part.

When the moons light touches my face or when the brick walls begin to close in around me, I'll keep running until I find you again. When the city signs call my name or when the midnight rhyme sings me to sleep, I'll remember your face.

These avenues will keep our secrets, protect them, and never break the oath; for every promise that's kissed our violent lips will be honored by the fate of the star-crossed eclipse.

PARLOR TRICKS

They'll never understand how it feels to love like this;

to move mountains and find the strength-

to hang onto a prayer and relinquish the outcome to fate,

knowing deep within that you'll come home.

I can promise you this:

I *never* want to feel this way for anyone else but *you*.

You are the storm

and the rainbow right after.

Your favorite color is clear

and honestly, *what the fuck does that even mean?*

Well, who cares..

I think it's perfect;

a perfect example of how your cryptic mind

keeps me on my toes;

how even the most damaged soul

can heal me better than anyone.

You don't make sense

most of the time,

and yet, I never understood someone

as much as you as I understand you.

Time is an illusion

or at least that's what some cheesy bastard once said.

But now, I think I believe em'.

'Cause with you, time doesn't just stop;

it disappears.

It merely doesn't exist

I hate it and adore it all at once.

And now, I think we have ourselves a problem.
You see, I'm *not* running from you.
In fact, I'm chasing
because I think
I'm actually pretty in love with you as it turns out.

What am I even saying?
This is what you do to me:

A parlor trick,
my life's most talented magician.
One minute you're here
and the next …gone;
leaving my heart wide open
with a dusting of your blueprint
scattered within me,
through and through
permanently.

BKLYN → LOWER EAST SIDE (CIRCA 2017)

The tracks begin to rumble, cautioning all to step back from the yellow line. Rebellious by nature, I lean forward, observing the faint light peeking out from the dark end of the tunnel. A fleeting dispersion of elation escapes me as the red "L" approaches faster and closer towards the station.

Of course, all the seats are filled, but that's okay- I enjoy to stand anyway. My hands latch tightly around the sweaty handlebar, leftover from someone before me. The germs, I don't mind. I'm always equipped with sanitizer. Everyone is along for the ride- some, longer than others, which gives me time to observe and scrutinize their varying behavior. I play this game in which I try to guess who will exit at each station and usually, I'm almost always correct. You can tell a lot about a person within just a few stops.

For example, there's a woman to my left in her late twenties at best, and she's secluded in her own world as she's eyes deep into a piece by Molière. Surely, she's a French lit major who overuses satire at dinner parties to help disguise the pain she feels. And later, she'll leave early, turn up intoxicated at a bar downtown, and complain to the bartender about how unfair life really is. Just a hunch, but I think she'll get off at Houston Street.

Sitting down in front of me, a man in his thirties looks distressed as he continues to press the "fuck you" button on some girl named "Tess." No really, that's her name and she must be a bitch, for anyone to strike out with this guy.

K. LA LUNE

Dressed to the nine and clean-shaven, his hands look tired, his forehead is sweaty. And as bold as I may be at times, it's just too crowded to shoot my shot, so when he looks my way, I'll offer a quirky nod. As for him, he'll exit at Prince Street, where he'll swipe his black American Express in exchange for a new luxury piece. Then he'll stroll into a pub close by, in his new disguise, and pretend he isn't "*that guy,*" all while still ignoring Tess.

That fucking bitch.

And lastly, in the corner, curled up with her knees against her chest, is someone with a striking resemblance to a girl I used to know; Chipped nails, all half-bitten, lost in a dream state as she writes away. Her overalls are covered in paint, hair tossed up messily, and when she looks up, we lock eyes and I feel as though I'm going to cry. Kindly, she offers a smile and resumes to her work. If she's anything like you know who… Canal Street. This one, I'm sure.

So, one by one, they begin to exit. Houston, Prince, and Canal Street.

The train then reaches its final stop but there's one more girl I'd like to tell you about. Judging by her dirty worn-out chucks and teary eyes, this one seems like she was just along for the ride. No destination in mind or place she needs to be. And, when the L empties, she'll take her seat, where she'll ride, observe, write, and repeat.

K. LA LUNE

A SOUL IN PROGRESS

Everyone you meet will have a different "view" of me, purposely crafted into far from normal perfection.

> For some, I'll speak only in a horrendous British accent, while I sip tea I don't "fancy" but pretend to for the sake of commitment.

During each era of my life, I'll select a specific skin to dress myself in, finding bits of me within the experience. There's a trail of breadcrumbs left behind- usually a lesson I embed within the notches of my crown.

i'll never be perfect but always in progress,

arising like a phoenix from the ash and debris around me. Privy to the secret languages of numbers and codes, birds and dragonflies, butterflies, even the sun, I'll always know which way to go- for a soul in progress always begins with a leap of faith, solidifying dreams into reality with the sheer sentiments of pure hope and divine acceptance.

PETRA TOU ROMIOU

Old legend once said that a grown maiden was birthed from the sea, drifting towards the coast of Paphos, Cyprus. The Greek Goddess of beauty and love, Aphrodite, emerged, born from sea foam. Admired by all, she was gifted the ability to seduce any man. Vain and green-eyed by nature, she was said to take the lives of any woman she felt possessed greater beauty than she.

Petra Tou Romiou, also known as "Aphrodite's Rock," stands tall off the shore of Cyprus, where if swam around counter-clockwise three times, one would procure eternal beauty. Another local legend swears that if one was to swim around the rock three times clockwise, their soul mate would appear.

In dreams, I'd often visit the beautiful Cyprus coast, where I'd dip my toes into the mythology of those beckoned at the will and call of Aphrodite. I'd swim laps around her rock as waves crashed into the surface- the outcry of seafoam roaring, bewildering me with a tale from long ago. I'd wish and wish for her belt of magic to appear- the one that was said to enchant anyone who'd wear it. In the distance, my soulmate would emerge from the depths with outstretched arms, inviting me into the sea where we'd live eternally.

GROWING UP WITH THE CITY

When I was sixteen, I'd quarrel with my parents as I'd beg them to allow me to ride the train into Manhattan *alone*- a taxing task for those whose voices are rarely ever heard.

As defiant as a teenager could be, I'd sneak away anyway, losing myself in a lucid screenplay as I wandered the city of concrete, endlessly.

Easily, I'd fall in love with the ambiance surrounding me- sundry elements, cultures, and people alike. I'd inject my DNA into the streets- atoms of my soul filling the avenues, marking my territory.

I'd memorize street signs and landmarks quickly as I'd tilt my head upward and watch buildings trail the sky to infinite heights. *One day, it's where I'd be.*

When I was seventeen, I'd climbed to one of the largest buildings in the entirety of the city. I was on top of the world as lights lit up, unfolding the world around me.

My lungs filled with air, saturating the oxygen with profound stupor. Forthgoing from there, I reserved that spot for only me and the memory to share. No friend or lover would be caught with me up there.

Throughout the years, I'd grown with the city- celebrating happy times, milestones, birthdays, and breakups.

K. LA LUNE

Tears would fall, burning into the ground below me, sending out a signal to the keeper of the streets that I was in need of some relief. I'd follow the trail to the closest bar, order the same old spiel, confess to a stranger how I ended up here.

In my late twenties, I became queen of the rooftops- various places where I found myself often. I'd scale to the greatest heights to feel the reign of glory that had always been rooted within me.

Tipping as close to the edge as possible, I'd spread my arms as wide as could be, feeling the magic of the night flow through my fingertips. I'd feel the rustle of wind sweep through my tousled hair, knotting it up instantly.

In those moments, *nothing else mattered.* I was born to rule these massive streets, allow them to speak to me in their hidden voice.

When hope felt dismal, I knew the places which would remind me of just how enchanted life could be when you've spent your whole life growing up with the city.

THE MANUSCRIPT

From a young age, I *knew* I was a visionary. Wild scenes, painted with sharpened-fine details, stretched me open, beaming straight through between my eyes and into my mind, coating each nerve with delicate visions- flashy and chromatic. I'd view the world through a kaleidoscope lens where everything was colossal and vibrant.

Even amidst darkened realities, bows and bands of color coiled around the shadows, turning displaced ruins into golden arches. I'd shut my eyes tighter, watching bursts of phosphorescent hues swim in harmony in the distance as vast vistas emerged from the mountainsides.

My mind is its own kind of artist- crafting experience with the naked eye, supraliminal to the delicacies of what's often overlooked.

With these abilities, I'm able to re-visit places, people, memories, as many times over as I'd like and never skip a beat. I could play, pause, rewind, and fast forward, while always preserving the details within the concrete.

My writing has no limits. I can jump as high as the clouds above me, dance with the stars as I'm tucked within Earth's orbit, or skate as fast as I can along the rings of Saturn. Failure cannot touch me when tapped into the rare oddity within me.

Every letter and every word would ooze a different color as it clung to the pages, preserving bits and pieces of me throughout.

The intricacy of details weaved profound memories through the ink as it dried, bonding itself forever. Saturated drippings of hyperboles hung to the corners of every exclamation, while answers and truth hid in the shadows of question marks.

I'd watch the sun rise and set for days on end as I perfected the manuscript, faultlessly coupled within my grasp. Careful not to bend the corners, I'd smooth over the crinkles bunching up at the edges.

Everything had to be perfect

Wary at times, many things are crossed out. Too much of me is etched and buried within the chapter and verse. Some days, I haggle with the success of it, for the manuscript, I may never finish with the stories that will never see the light of day.

this too shall pass

this too shall pass | the ebbs & flows of a journey

THIS BODY

This body doesn't feel like mine- its bones protruding, making contact with skin; visible to those who come near. I compensate with baggy fits, disguising my disgust at what lies beneath, tempted to fill it with the stuffing of these clothes that fall from my shoulders. I swear, I'm as light as a feather and as frail as dust from a gentle touch, swept away and left to wither to nothing.

THE THOUGHTS

The thoughts, they come- hurling through the cityscape of this jarring lens, filling the already half-empty glass with more ridicule, more blasphemy suggesting to let it all go; her, us- the idea spun amidst a heavenly web, routing me towards destiny, following a satirical string of signs, pulling me towards her direction. I'm submissive to my intuition, falling into its seduction of magic as it propels me towards far-out lands; a place unseen on roadside maps or Plymouths out west. "You're crazy," they say, *the thoughts* that is, feeding me jagged pills of fallacies that try to convince me that that these musings are nothing but fairytale endings, fooling me of what's real and what isn't inside of my head.

WHAT I FEAR MOST

Sweaty hands, rosy cheeks stolen from a pale complexion, and a shadowy hand choked around my neck, feeding me violent thoughts and forceful visions of what I fear most- death. I'm afraid to die; afraid that I walk along the rickety hands of the clock like a circus performer amongst a tightrope, falling to my demise in meadows of unknowing whereabouts.

I'm obsessed with death, romanticizing the fragility of these love notes pocketed between the valves of my heart- their silent words buried alongside a hollowed body within a blackened space of nothing.

I'm afraid to die; losing my memories to another life, no resonance of who I used to be, how my face looked, how I liked my tea- precious moments fading beneath a breach of time and reality.

I spit shards of eventful inevitabilities, unable to swallow the jagged thoughts eroding the present, constructing cages around the beauty of life as I suffer at the mercy of what I can't control.

SHACKLED TO DOUBT

These thoughts gnawed away at my soul, picking at crumbling bone protruding from a disastrous pile of broken hope- a precursor to knotted emotions drowning amongst a sea of wasted days spent longing for you; a hideaway amidst the thick of a cavernous trench, picking petals from flowers as dead as the fires that once kept me warm.

I'm throttled within the blunt force trauma of time knocking me from one minute to the next, punishing the moments stolen by the inexorable decay of life peeling away. I'm banging on the shell of an opal glass sphere, barring my pleas to suspend these unforgiving nights that keep me shackled to a lone post in the heart of nowhere.

But all is silent; even these lips have run dry, my words shriveled up like raisins in the sand, while the light within begins to dim-losing its flicker over and over again.

WHAT TROUBLES ME MOST

I'm kept awake at nights wondering if, *she too*, lays with her eyes fixed amongst the void, curious of the same. It's then that I feel a raucous wave of *everything I want to say, everything I need for her to hear*, begin to teem with fury- as though too much time is passing, that all these jumbled thoughts and words and feelings will keep building until the pressure cooks too greatly, and I self-implode; losing her to her fears- an adversary that punishes fate, overshadowing the beauty of something written in the stars. But, I know *she knows*- I'm absolutely certain, and I think that's what troubles me the most.

CAUGHT IN LIMBO

The contents inside of my mind

teeter in limbo,

jumping from AM to FM,

coasting amongst the airwaves

as I tune in to listen to the secret gateway

that houses a poetic pulse;

percussive clamor like that of a tangled terrarium of static

that teems in between wavy outbursts and solemn wishes-

the Mozart of chaotic rhymes and spilled guts

worth of nothing inside.

GAMBLING WITH FATE

Gambling with the pursuit, I'm heavy in the eyes, fighting the urge to back away from these flames- fiery infernos bridging the gap between us, holding our tongues hostage, our words fettered. Amongst these lines that trail my body, each one leads me to you-swarming with lifetimes of memories unable to be touched, unable to be tasted, even when I crave to feel the emotions that exist somewhere down under. I'd wait a million more days to see the sun rise from the western sky, where oceans collide and your smile satisfies; the sweetest of misery basked in pools of honey-a sultry duality rallying a monster from within, leading to the parts that eternally bind me to you.

TOO SOON

It's a shame- all the years spent tormented in a raucous storm of hate; hate for myself, my past, my mistakes- the scabs I'd pick at until there was no skin left; all the blood left to pool and oxidize as the years peeled me away.

At twenty-five, *I was infinite*, yet I never knew it- believing the howling words surging windspeed within me, taking ownership of what they wanted me to believe- that I was frail, weak, too curious for my own good.

But, as it turned out,

i was none of those things

Fiercely and unapologetically wild, I once soared alongside moonbeams, shining amidst darkened shadows that only tried to cloak my radiance with a lackluster smile; dimming an innocence I had retired to my youth, never once realizing how precious the rhythm of a soulful heart really is- pure moments stolen away by the pungent aftertaste of growing up too soon.

A FALL FROM GRACE

Falling from grace,
I'm cushioned in an alluring halcyon,
redolent of sunshine
dripping warmth from its rays;
for these clouds, they smile in shades of gray
holding their streams,
allowing me to imbue
beyond their hazy masses
in hopes to show me
that in lieu of stormy uncertainties,
these soldiering bones
carry more of what
these shadows try to fool me of.

K. LA LUNE

ACCEPTANCE

I've loosened the holster, once strapped to the thick of my thighs-
forging through life with control at my fingertips.

Sleepless twilights and dazed-filled sunny days, I allowed my
energy to drain like a battery on overdrive, stealing my time for
the sake of being 'right.'

I'd write the story until it was nearly perfect; dotting my 'I's' and
crossing my 'T's', making certain that I was the author who get
her happy ending.

I'd sweep my breadcrumbs, erase the trail of inadequacies, falling
victim to exhaustion and all the taxing things that came along
with it.

I was indebted to checking off every box, fixing the script,
repainting the set, firing the extras who'd taunt me with lack.

I made contact with peace as she'd whisper reassurance, pulling
me from these grips. "*Surrender and be present.*"

MELANCHOLY BLUES

I've cycled through life, viewing the world through a rose-bombed lens. Around me, faces and places grew from wild Junipers, casting all my hearts wishes in the shape of my initials.

The world was my stage! And the stars were my lights! And the planets, they'd shine at every marvel I'd create! My life was a carousal of beauty and I was lucky. But time slipped and the dark found me, veiling these eyes, covering them in sinister shades of melancholy blue.

I stopped smiling, forgot how to laugh, how to dress, how to act. I was clouded with fears, fears of death and what happens next. For fuck sake, I'm only thirty! "It'll pass," I'd assure myself, unaware of how strong the thoughts would continue to persist, cycling through every scenario, every deceptive terror banging at my door.

I started to become obsessed with these nagging wonders, fearing the inevitable stranger who'd come for me eventually. I was stuck in an unforgiving tsunami, fearing dying; which only inhibited me from living.

THIRTY YEARS

For thirty years, I've watched seasons peel away, watched my face change, and my baby hairs turn gray. I've cooked under pressure in the most unsettling places, turned ash into gold, speckled myself with the dust of all my mistakes.

For thirty years, I've painted my room all shades and colors from pewter to alabaster- standing out as I stuck to the walls, awaiting for someone to take notice. I'm subdued in the reveries of times' faulty grips, romanticizing my life and what I've so far done with it.

For thirty years, I never once feared my existence and how much was left of it. Now, it's all this mind can think about; forging through murky waters of hypothetical bruises- leaving me in the thick of disillusioned scenarios, keeping me from living.

NOT ALL SUNSHINE

My legs dangle, creating divots in the pool water beneath me. A hardened reflection ripples and I push all washed out tropes of my past away, watching it drift and never return.

I'm idle in a space of limbo, feeling everything while feeling nothing- nerve endings comatose, staring blankly at the metaphorical road ahead of me. I feel for the sun, who tries to soothe me in warmth, reassuring me that all will be alright if I promise her a smile.

But, I'm bitter and I'm angry, and I just can't stand to watch both feet stand placid any longer. My heart is aching to move as it screams and pounds relentlessly, losing its vivacity each time my mind shuts off, hibernating in a state of loss for what feels like an eternity.

K. LA LUNE

SLEEPY PILLS

I rely on these pills to make me sleepy- help my mind to coast adrift off the sea, where turbulence peaks, jolting my bones, leaving them to rattle with the currents.

I stare at the ominous void beveled above my head, conjuring sheep that don't even exist, checking off every dream that's failed to procure its wish. I'm tossing and turning, these sheets are now messy, and I'm doubled down in a symphony of anxiety, raising my pressure with its agonizing clamor.

These voices won't hush, even when I "shush." I'm now afloat in my own sweat, hoping to drown within its slimy depths. And then it hits me, I'm thirty, and there's no going back.

A frazzled mind, mine begins to implode; steam pumping from a crisis overdrive. Give me a watch, a clock, anything to turn back time! I want to be twenty- when I was wild, young, and unapologetically happy- joyously perplexed by the simplest fruits of this life, never fearing thirty or the depressive realizations that would follow along with it.

ALL ABOARD THE TRAIN TO NO MAN'S LAND

Boarding the train to no-man's land, I add a pep to my step, cruising along the tracks as I escape the formidable changes that have gnawed away at my soul.

The rumblings of the wheels drown out the pulsing haste that pounds like a sledge hammer at the walls of my chest. I'm apprehensive to jump, to take a risk and free myself, but I know deep inside, it's the only way out of this mental state of mind.

SPILLED MILK

Perceiving mistakes often transmutes to "*making mountains out of molehills*." Unconsciously, we stitch ourselves within the jeering jolts of the engine keeping that "mistake" afloat.

Harvesting our self-worth within this notion of destruction, enables one to stay submerged, forever stuck looming above within the shadows.

After all, most mistakes are only spilled milk- it happens, clean it up, and move on.

Throughout the years, I'd dive headfirst into the waves and allow for them to keep me suffocating beneath the water, while the solution shined above the surface.

Within my mindset, I kept myself buried, consistently putting myself in the face of agony, while forgetting that lessons can be learned quite easily… *when you learn to forgive yourself.*

CHANGE YOUR STORY

I'd spent years on a crash course of my own self-implosion, skinning myself raw with mistakes that I once deemed detrimental to my existence.

Nights were unforgiving in wake of my solace, gutting knives into my back and side at the mere thought of what, *I had believed*, I'd lost.

But, it was I who secured the deadbolts around my wrists, imprisoning myself in all the things I couldn't change, regretful of the moments in which I wish I wasn't my own worst enemy.

I was sunk in a plot that only needed to be re-written; polish the character who fell amongst too many faults, unaware of her own powerful emergence in the thick of the forest.

No longer would I paint my soul with diluted shades of pewter and gray; only repellant of the vitality blossoming around the cage in which I harbored my essence, my purpose, my divine grace.

ACCEPTANCE PT II

There's no greater treasure than the art of letting what's meant
to be find you; knees deep in marshy waters, sinking with the
ebbs of the earth, allowing its plan to rise as you ascend-

a mastery of acceptance

VENOMOUS TOUCH

I can only dance with her ghostly touch for so long,

until it begins to feel more like an ache,

more like a sting *sinking deep with no relief.*

epilogue

epilogue | spoiler alert: she finds her most authentic self in the chaos

SO CLOSE, BUT SO FAR AWAY

Pain- deadweight thinning my blood, emptying from the keyholes punctured amidst my heart.

> *She's always there inside of me*, but tonight, I'm pinned down by a lonely touch; a tear-stained stitch of loss leaving me to sit idle with these sorrow-tuned thoughts.

In the isle of my core, I call out her name- a rickety shrill anointed in misery; a lost voice buried amidst a void. Surely, *she can feel* my tears running untamed behind her eyes, while her absence grows and swallows me; sinking me deeper, losing my sense of why I hold her so tight.

K. LA LUNE

AN INNOCENT DESIRE

Seedlings of romance sprout behind the penumbra of what once left her bitter. Buried beneath the deepest thrush of her fears, she finds a key to unlocking treasures of wild dreams-opulent ruins holding storybook endings; delicate and poetically supple- a place to bare her soul in bountiful daylight, taking flight in relishing in a wish come true; a hearts most innocent desire.

FINALLY (MAYBE ONE DAY)

Finally, who would have thought? Surely, not me. I'm struggling to understand how powerful fate is when she's sitting across from me at a dinner table on the Lower East Side, waiting for one of us to speak.

But, I'm lost in the everglades that drip honey from its caves- the universe that stares back at me from the universe behind her eyes.

I'm blushing- she's caught me looking… *staring even*, at her pouty lips, parted slightly.

It's strange; as though I'm staring into the looking glass- a mirror of my own heart.

She's smirking and my upper lip starts to curve too. I'm shy and I'm curious of this ghost who resembles everything that I am, yet, beats to a different drum than me.

Quietly, I shush my heart- it's eager, beating too loudly; surely, she must hear it, or worse, *feel it*. This thing is jolting me like an avalanche, sending reverberations of chaos, quaking once it reaches its medium.

"How long have you known?" I ask, catching her off guard for only a moment.

"I've always kind of known, you know?" she's thinking, I can feel it- the chattering of her mind computing memories of 'firsts,' translating them into a sonorous orchestra of truths all piling into my heart at once. "It was always just this *knowing*."

Nodding my head in full understanding, we both allow the silent knowing to speak in lieu of the words that could never begin to honor the power of an eternal-bound connection.

"Every night, I would see you in my dreams. For a long time, I thought I was crazy. I'd do everything... *anything*, to push away the truth of what I'd been running from for years."

Pausing, she collects her pain- parts of her silent tongue that she views as mistakes; years of running, hiding... avoiding- yet undeniably drawn to the desire; an ache so debilitating when it begins to burrow and fester underneath your skin, peeling your senses until you've been pried wide open, unable to hide from the truth any longer.

"The dreams are so real and I feel safe when you're near. I think I ran because I was afraid I'd lose the power in that one day, when I closed my eyes, I'd be standing here alone... a time where the fantasy of you would no longer follow."

A STATE OF BEING

....

Silence, lulling its sweet charm, pocketing peace deep within; a miracle destination, once shadowed by an obtuse satirical clause of view.

Here, I can breathe without the soot to bury my lungs in haste, suffocating at the mercy of time slipping away. I'm enveloped in my own journey, in the warm embrace of this new state of being; a paradise to accept what is, what isn't, what may never be, and what is meant to be.

The moon smiles as she winks in my direction, acknowledging where I've been and how loyal I've been in holding her secrets- tightening the clasp like a promise caged within a locket; a sentiment that I've worn like armor amidst the storms.

"*Daughter*," she claims, hugging me in her midnight glow, bestowing honor upon the heart that I once hid behind bereaving shadows; a wall I built around my name, locking myself within wrought iron fences, afraid of letting pieces of me slip away.

"Eye on the prize," I once used to say, focusing success on the destiny of what will one day be. I sought answers of the future in the wrong spaces, peering behind stone walls that only ruptured when misaligned with what mattered.

I found that destiny isn't a place, but rather a state of being- an accumulation of emotions that have been wrung out to dry;

K. LA LUNE

twisting and prodding the excess dampness, pulverizing the contents to quicken under pressure.

I now leave the haste to mull under the eyes of day break, having found the key to peace in the gentle hums of simply "just being."

I FELL OUT OF LOVE WITH NEW YORK CITY

There was an impending change that loomed over me as I walked the streets that once collected my soul- a monumental place that I held high on a pedestal.

Being back in New York City- a place, a sanctuary that's carved its charm into my eyes, has now left a sour taste; a flavor I'd never imagined that would linger and swallow me in a vortex of bitterness.

It didn't feel great; I'll tell you that much as I still search for the perfect words to detail the clouds rolling in above my head. It felt very much the same as having a fight with an old friend, then seeing them in public some months later. Or hearing a song that you once sang and dedicated to someone you loved who then broke your heart.

"*But I love Manhattan*," I muttered to myself, frazzled by an array of chattering emotions burying me with heavy thoughts that only complicated my internal world further .

As I walked the streets, I was lost in a trance- a limbo state of being as the new me stepped into the skin of the old, never realizing how empty and cold my heart really felt each time; how it *never really* made me feel complete; how it *never truly* soothed my aching bones.

While suspended some absurd amount of feet off the ground, I stared into the window of the city's soul, engaging in a mournful heart to heart. With this new lens, I was puzzled by... *not what I saw*, but rather, *what I didn't see*- this perfect escape of a world I'd painted with my pain; a place I injected with a disillusioned cure, a quick fix, holding memories of you in its hands.

The sky was no longer bright or filled with the special pantone of my mind. It cried in shades of black and gray, while the clouds wrapped its grips around my neck like a stranger securing me to strings attached to my wrists; a decaying puppet whose opening act was long overdue to close.

It was then that reality struck me- a hardened truth striking me unapologetically:

I poured a piece of you into every crack in the sidewalk, every window of every building of every soul I'd pass on the street. I left crumbs of you each place I stepped, in every tip I left and signed my name to, and in every drink I'd slug down to numb the confusion surrounding you.

 This concrete jungle was a conduit or maybe even a "horcrux"- something I never sought out to do, but accidentally created *because of missing you*.

Without you, I felt incomplete and sad.

When I chased the high of the city lights, those pieces of you that I once sprinkled, found me like a drug, and in turn began killing me slowly.

I was never addicted to the city. *I was addicted to the feelings it fed me;* a codependent escape from facing the truth reflected in this shattered mirror:

>that you were not the answer to my withering unhappiness and no amount of time feigning for another taste was going to heal the void prodding from the depths of my being.

I fell out of love with New York City but instead, I found a loving home somewhere close by- a place I never had to search any further than the warming treasure deep inside.

In the three year absence, I'd been forced to carry the weight of my own volitions, tend to my gardens and weather the storms. I learned that my journey was a piece of art that needed new and expansive colors- colors that came from the heat of all that I was and everything that I wasn't, and not the dismal façade that I once thought kept me warm.

New York City was a house but not a home: a tower I was meant to build and detonate when the message became more clear and revealed itself in time.

A SHIFT IN LOVE

Often, I'm drowning in an abyss of poetry that speak fiercely from behind her eyes- poignant treasures swimming freely in each soulful stare, blinking sharply in my direction; an ephemeral moment that comes and then goes-

a wild trance of limerence,

taking me by the hand to far out lands of wild vistas that unravel from these stories, wrapped in moonbeams, leaving her mind.

Demure in nature, yet chaotic at heart, each fragile piece that chips away and emotes with free spirit, kidnaps my vision, painting my world with the flick of her brush; a shift in narrative to match her unyielding view of love.

STILL / ALWAYS

I'd be a damn fool to let her walk out of my life for a second time without screaming, *"it's always been you,"* at the top of my lungs, allowing my voice to pervade through even the toughest of layers.

The words would bellow from my core with enough blast to defy the laws of science; so much so that the vacuum of silence in space wouldn't be enough to keep my feelings quiet.

I've *always* loved her- this lifetime and every lifetime before. And I don't care what may have happened between us in other lives to keep us away from each other. I *won't* let that happen this time around, because despite how much time has passed and how much my heart has ached to vomit up all my feelings, words still fail me when she's standing right in front of me.

"*Still?*" they ask in response to my love, as though the words are dispelled in a foreign language that I can't understand. I pause, ruminating on how to describe the feeling, knowing there's an entire story of its own inside that word. They're looking for a simple 'yes' or 'no,' but the gravity behind that answer is so much heavier than they can ever understand.

'Still,' as though I'd be able to so easily forget her, move on, fall in love with someone else- as though my love for her could be bandaged with a little bit of peroxide and a band aid- as if time and love are linear- as though I'm the author who could erase the past and re-write the ending. For me, 'still' *is* 'always.'

.

The thing about her and I is that we speak in words that cannot be heard with the ears. Our soul just knows. *It feels.* It wreaks havoc, dismantles the foundation, crumbles the debris in the tiny grips of all we can't hold... It yearns for what it lacks, except, what it lacks is nothing at all.

Our love loops and weaves between the atoms in the air, the constellations in our sky, and most importantly, it teaches us that love, *no matter how painful*, is the price we pay to feel. And feeling is the greatest gift a soul can receive.

ALL THE THINGS I SHOULD HAVE SAID THEN

You left just as fast as you arrived...

I wondered about you,
about Us,
about the peculiarity of our connection;

how it made me feel as though magic was real
and that *we* are the *living proof* in it.

I wrote you every day for 4 years-
a piece of me sealed but never sent,
hoping my pleas would be heard
and someone above would grant me my wish;

To see you,
feel you,
say sorry for all the things

i should have said then

K. LA LUNE

31 CANDLES

Spinning, spinning, spinning ... the hands of the clock, the pull of the world siphoned in the grips of gravity's kiss. I'm resistant to cave in; to make peace with the seasons of my life that come and go, forever changing and rearranging.

I fucking miss being twenty-six and the lack of care for consequence that swam along with it. I miss the cheesy sentiment in "the sky is the limit," now held bound in a gruesome chokehold that I already believe I've seen- peaked and fleeted in the span of what feels like a few minutes.

I'm nursing my age as though it's a spherical ball sculpted and held in the smalls of my hands; wary of time punishing me quicker with each year that passes.

The world around me has grown more quiet; distilled like water in a pond on a warmly-stagnant evening. And yet, my mind explodes with a myriad of words; some in a language that I've never heard, but that I understand by the feelings that hold them in a centripetal embrace.

I'm now 31 and I mourn the years that have shaped my essence, afraid that if I blink for *even another second*, I'll turn around and fade to nothing.

But, I'm willing to erase this limiting piece of me; allow what's meant to be to guide me along the way- easing the habit to control, to enjoy the once in a lifetime magic of the *unknown*.

K. LA LUNE

BREAKING AWAY FROM THIS COCOON

If I could go back in time and change anything, *I wouldn't.*
Every person and situation was meant to poke, prod, and expel
my soul from its cocoon, to give me my wings,

so I can finally fly.

I'm just a misfit amongst the jungle in the

city that never sleeps

thank you.

About the Author

K. La Lune is an American poet, whose art is inspired by the magic of a spiritual connection. Born and raised in Manhattan, the city that never sleeps holds a clandestine grip on her work, just as her name pays homage to the moon- a muse that will never grow old.

Author of
"Mirror, Mirror" and *"She Loves Me, She Loves Me Not"*
www. iamklalune.com ; @k. la_lune

table of

unhinged chaos

"do it anyway" 1

I just don't give a fuck 2

the woman who couldn't see, saw me 3

puppet 5

get on your knees and pray 6

a spiritual awakening 7

down the rabbit hole 8

that's the thing about sobriety 9

expiration date 10

an insatiable craving for a broken heart 11

ruby red slippers 12

looking for ever-after 13

temple of the soul 14

zoning out 15

poetic agony killed the poet 16

red pill of shame 17

blacked out on the 7:56 express 19

eternal bond of forever 23

24 /7 24

a promise never kept 25

mirage of the night 26

onward and upward to oblivion 27

A LITTLE BIT OF EVERYTHING
ALL WRAPPED UP INTO ONE MESSY BOOK OF UNHINGED CHAOS

Printed in Great Britain
by Amazon